INSTRUCTOR'S MANUAL

to accompany

Fluid Power With Applications

Fourth Edition

by

Anthony Esposito

Prentice Hall

Upper Saddle River, New Jersey   Columbus, Ohio

Printed in the United States of America

10 9 8 7 6 5 4 3 2 1

ISBN: 0-13-566027-0

CONTENTS

PREFACE

The purpose of this manual for FLUID POWER WITH APPLICATIONS is threefold:

1. To provide the instructor with student-oriented learning objectives for each chapter. In this way the instructor can better organize teaching strategies and testing techniques.

2. To provide the instructor with answers to textbook questions which are designed to give the student the necessary practice for understanding the important concepts and applications.

3. To provide the instructor with solutions to textbook problems which are designed to give the student the necessary practice for mastering sound problem solving techniques.

Many of the textbook exercises (questions and problems) can be adapted directly for student testing purposes.

I hope that this manual will help the instructor to more effective use the Textbook so that he or she can provide the student with a better education in the vast subject of Fluid Power.

Anthony Esposito

PART I   OVERVIEW OF TEXT OBJECTIVES

CHAPTER 1   INTRODUCTION TO FLUID POWER

This chapter introduces the student to the overall field of
fluid power. It answers the question "What is fluid power?" and
presents a corresponding historical background. Advantages and
applications of fluid power systems are discussed in detail.
Emphasis is placed on the fact that fluid power systems are
designed to perform useful work. A complete hydraulic system and
a complete pneumatic system are individually presented with
identifications of the necessary components and their functions.
The fluid power industry is examined in terms of its bright,
expanding future and the great need for fluid power mechanics,
technicians and engineers. Environmental issues dealing with
developing biodegradable fluids, reducing oil leakage and
reducing noise levels are discussed as challenges and
opportunities facing the fluid power industry.

CHAPTER 2   PROPERTIES OF HYDRAULIC FLUIDS

This chapter deals with the single most important material
in a hydraulic system: the working fluid. It introduces the
student to the various types of hydraulic and pneumatic fluids
and their most important properties for fluid power applications.
The differences between liquids and gases is outlined in terms of
fundamental characteristics and applications. Methods for testing
for the various fluid properties (such as bulk modulus,
viscosity, viscosity index, oxidation and corrosion resistance,
fire resistance, lubricating ability and neutralization number)
are presented. The student is introduced to Pascal's Law where
the concepts of pressure, head and force are developed. Units in
the Metric System are described and compared to units in the
English System. This will prepare the student for the inevitable
United States adoption of the Metric System. Methods for properly
maintaining and disposing of hydraulic fluids are discussed in
terms of accomplishing pollution control and conservation of
natural resources objectives.

CHAPTER 3   ENERGY AND POWER IN HYDRAULIC SYSTEMS

This chapter lays the groundwork for the material covered in subsequent chapters. It introduces the student to the basic laws and principles of fluid mechanics which are necessary for understanding the concepts presented in later chapters. Emphasis is placed on energy, power, efficiency, continuity of flow, Pascal's Law and Bernoulli's Theorem. Stressed is the fact that fluid power is not a source of energy but, in reality, is an energy transfer system. As such, fluid power should be used in applications where it can transfer energy better than other systems. Application presented include the hydraulic jack and the air-to-hydraulic pressure booster. Energy, power and flow rate units are compared between the English and Metric Systems. Problem solving techniques are presented using both the English and Metric Systems.

CHAPTER 4   THE DISTRIBUTION SYSTEM

This chapter introduces the student to the various types of conductors and fittings used to conduct the fluid between the various components of a fluid power system. Advantages and disadvantages of the four primary types of conductors (steel pipe, steel tubing, plastic tubing and flexible hose) are discussed along with practical applications. Sizing and pressure rating techniques are presented using English and Metric units. The very important distinction between burst pressure and working pressure is emphasized as related to the concept of factor of safety. The difference between tensile stress and tensile strength is also explained. Precautions are emphasized for proper installation of conductors to minimize maintenance problems after a fluid power system is placed into operation. The design, operation and application of quick disconnect couplings are also presented.

CHAPTER 5   BASICS OF HYDRAULIC FLOW IN PIPES

This chapter investigates the mechanism of energy losses due to friction associated with the flow of a fluid inside a pipeline. It introduces the student to laminar and turbulent flow, Reynold's Number and frictional losses in fittings as well as pipes. Hydraulic circuit analysis by the equivalent length method is presented. Stressed is the fact that it is very important to keep all energy losses in a fluid power system to a minimum acceptable level. This requires the proper selection of the sizes of all pipes and fittings used in the system. The computer analysis of hydraulic systems is presented as a means of optimizing the performance of complete hydraulic systems. The use of computers permits an expedient cost-benefit analysis to be made of any proposed system parameter change, taking into account long term effects. An example is the oxidation of the oil due to excessive temperatures resulting from increased frictional energy losses if, for example, a smaller diameter pipe is used in an attempt to reduce costs. Also discussed are flow and pressure measuring devices used to trouble-shoot hydraulic systems. Problem solving techniques are presented using both the English and Metric Systems.

CHAPTER 6   THE SOURCE OF HYDRAULIC POWER: PUMPS

This chapter introduces the student to the operation of pumps which convert mechanical energy into hydraulic energy. The theory of pumping is presented for both positive displacement and non-positive displacement pumps. Emphasized is the fact that pumps do not pump pressure but instead produce the flow of a fluid. The resistance to this flow, produced by the hydraulic system, is what determines the pressure. The operation and applications of the three principal types of fluid power pumps (gear, vane and piston) are described in detail. Methods are presented for selecting pumps and evaluating their performance using Metric and English units. The causes of pump noise are discussed and ways to reduce noise levels are identified. Also discussed are the design, operation and application of pressure intensifiers.

CHAPTER 7   FLUID POWER ACTUATORS

This chapter introduces the student to energy output devices (called actuators) which include cylinders and motors. Cylinders are linear actuators, whereas motors are rotary actuators. Emphasized is the fact that fluid power actuators perform just the opposite function of that performed by pumps. Thus actuators extract energy from a fluid and convert it into a mechanical output to perform useful work. Included are discussions on the construction, operation and applications of various types of hydraulic cylinders and motors. Presented is the mechanics of determining hydraulic cylinder loadings when using various linkages such as first class, second class and third class lever systems. Methods are presented for evaluating the performance of hydraulic motors using Metric as well as English units and selecting motors for various applications. Hydrostatic transmissions are discussed in terms of their practical applications as adjustable speed drives.

CHAPTER 8   CONTROL COMPONENTS IN HYDRAULIC SYSTEMS

This chapter introduces the student to the basic operations of control devices. It emphasizes the fact that control components must be properly selected or the entire hydraulic system will not function as required. The three basic types of control devices are: directional control valves, pressure control valves and flow control valves. Each type of valve is discussed in terms of its construction, operation and application. Emphasis is placed on the importance of knowing the primary function and operation of the various types of control components. This type of knowledge is not only required for designing a good functioning system, but it also leads to the discovery of innovative ways to improve a fluid power system for a given application. This is one of the biggest challenges facing the fluid power system designer. Also discussed as control components are the functions and operational characteristics of servo valves, cartridge valves, hydraulic fuses, pressure and temperature switches and shock absorbers.

CHAPTER 9   HYDRAULIC CIRCUIT DESIGN AND ANALYSIS

The material presented in previous chapters dealt with basic fundamentals and system components. This chapter is designed to offer insight into the basic types of hydraulic circuits including their capabilities and performance. The student should be made aware that when analyzing or designing a hydraulic circuit, three important considerations must be taken into account: (1) Safety of operation, (2) Performance of desired function, and (3) Efficiency of operation. This chapter provides an excellent opportunity for the student to use the computer to make an analysis of the performance of hydraulic systems. In order to properly understand the operation of hydraulic circuits, the student must have a working knowledge of components in terms of their operation and their ANSI graphical representations. This chapter also introduces the student to the various types of accumulators and accumulator circuits.

CHAPTER 10   PNEUMATICS - AIR PREPARATION AND COMPONENTS

This chapter introduces the student to pneumatics where pressurized gases (normally air) are used to transmit and control

4

power. Properties of air are discussed and the perfect gas laws are presented. Then the purpose, construction and operation of compressors are described. Methods are presented to determine the power required to drive compressors and the consumption rate of pneumatically driven equipment such as impact wrenches, hoists, drills, hammers, paint sprayers and grinders. Fluid conditioners such as filters, regulators, lubricators, mufflers and air dryers are discussed in detail. The student is then introduced to the design, operation and application of pneumatic pressure control valves, flow control valves, directional control valves and actuators (linear and rotary).

CHAPTER 11   PNEUMATICS - CIRCUITS AND APPLICATIONS

This chapter delves into the operation and analysis of basic pneumatic circuits and with corresponding applications. A comparison is made between hydraulic and pneumatic systems including advantages, disadvantages and types of applications. It is important for the student to appreciate the performance, operating characteristics, cost and application differences between pneumatic and hydraulic systems. The operation of pneumatic vacuum systems is discussed along with the analysis method for determining vacuum lift capacities. Techniques for evaluating the cost of air leakage into the atmosphere and frictional energy losses are presented. Methods are also provided for performing an analysis of accumulator systems. In addition, the trouble shooting of pneumatic circuits is discussed as a means of determining the causes of system malfunction. This chapter provides an excellent opportunity for the student to use the computer to optimize the performance of pneumatic systems.

CHAPTER 12   FLUID LOGIC CONTROL SYSTEMS

This chapter introduces students to the theory and operation of MPL (Moving Part Logic) and fluidic control systems. It is pointed out that successful miniaturization of MPL devices and also maintenance-free operation have resulted in increased utilization of MPL controls for a wide variety of industrial fluid power applications. Stressed is the fact that MPL and fluidics are used for controlling fluid power systems. As such, the MPL or fluidic portion of the system is the brains and the fluid power portion provides the brawn or muscle. Discussed in detail are the advantages and disadvantages of MPL and fluidic control systems as compared to electronic control systems. Illustrations, graphical symbols and truth tables are provided to give the student a better understanding of how MPL and fluidic

5

control devices function. Examples of MPL and fluidic logic
circuits are presented to illustrate the numerous practical
applications. Included are fluid logic circuits using general
logic symbols and the application of logic systems design
techniques using Boolean Algebra.

CHAPTER 13   ELECTRICAL CONTROLS FOR FLUID POWER CIRCUITS

This chapter introduces the student to circuits where
electrical devices are used for controlling fluid power. In
recent years, the trend has been toward electrical control of
fluid power systems and away from manual control. One reason for
this trend is that more machines are being designed for automatic
operation to be controlled with electrical signals from
computers. There are seven basic electrical devices which are
commonly used: manually actuated switches, limit switches,
pressure switches, solenoids, relays, timers and temperature
switches. By the use of a simple push button switch, an operator
can cause sophisticated equipment to perform complex operations.
Each type of electrical device is discussed in terms of its
construction, operation and function in various practical fluid
power applications. The theory, analysis and operation of
electro-hydraulic servo systems are also presented. Such a system
is closed-loop and, thus, provides very precise control of the
movement of actuators.

This chapter also introduces the student to the application
of programmable logic controllers (PLCs) for the control of fluid
power systems. Unlike general purpose computers, PLCs are
designed to operate in industrial environments where high ambient
temperature and humidity levels may exist as is typically the
case for fluid power applications. Unlike electro-mechanical
relays, PLCs are not hard-wired to perform specific functions.
Thus when system operating requirements change, a PLC software
program is readily changed instead of having to physically re-
wire relays.

CHAPTER 14   FLUID POWER MAINTENANCE AND SAFETY

This chapter stresses the need for planned preventative
maintenance. In the early years of fluid power systems,
maintenance was frequently performed on a hit and miss basis. The
prevailing attitude was to fix the problem when the system broke
down. However, with today's highly sophisticated machinery and
the advent of mass production, industry can no longer afford to
operate on this basis. The cost of downtime is prohibitive. In

this chapter the student is introduced to the common causes of
hydraulic system breakdown. Stressed is the fact that over half
of all hydraulic system problems have been traced directly to the
fluid. The mechanism of the wear of mating moving parts due to
solid particle contamination of the fluid, are discussed in
detail. Also explained are the problems caused by the existence
of gases in the hydraulic fluid. Components which are presented
include sealing devices, reservoirs, filters, strainers and heat
exchangers. Methods for trouble-shooting fluid power circuits are
described. Emphasized is the need for human safety when systems
are designed, installed, operated and maintained. The basic rule
to follow is "There should be no compromise when it comes to the
health and safety of people at the place of their employment."

PART II   ANSWERS AND SOLUTIONS TO TEXT EXERCISES

CHAPTER 1   INTRODUCTION TO FLUID POWER

1-1.   1. Steers and brakes automobiles.
       2. Moves earth.
       3. Harvests crops.
       4. Mines coal.
       5. Drives machine tools.

1-2.   Liquids provide a very rigid medium for transmitting power
       and thus can provide huge forces to move loads with utmost
       accuracy and precision.

1-3.   Advantages of Fluid Power Systems
       1. Not hindered by geometry of machine.
       2. Provides remote control.
       3. Complex mechanical linkages are eliminated.
       4. Instantly reversible motion.
       5. Automatic protection against overloads.
       6. Infinitely variable speed control.

       Advantages of Mechanical System:
       1. No mess due to oil leakage problems.
       2. No danger of bursting of hydraulic lines.
       3. No fire hazard due to oil leaks.

1-4.   Pascal's Law. The significance is that pressure is
       transmitted undiminished in a confined body of fluid.

1-5.   Hydraulic fluid power uses liquids which provide a very
       rigid medium for transmitting power. Thus huge forces can
       be provided to move loads with utmost accuracy and
       precision. Pneumatic systems exhibit spongy
       characteristics due to the compressibility of air. However
       pneumatic systems are less expensive to build and operate.

1-6.   Fluid power is the technology which deals with the
       generation, control and transmission of power using
       pressurized fluids.

1-7.   Hydraulic cylinder.

1-8.   Hydraulic motor.

8

1-9.   1. Liquids provide a very rigid medium.
        2. Power capacity of fluid systems is limited only by the
           strength capacity of the component material.

1-10.   Pneumatic systems exhibit spongy characteristics due to
        the compressibility of air.

1-11.   An electric motor or other power source to drive the pump
        or compressor.

1-12.   1. Reservoir.
        2. Pump.
        3. Prime mover.
        4. Valves.
        5. Actuators.
        6. Piping.

1-13.   1. Compressed air tank.
        2. Compressor.
        3. Prime mover.
        4. Valves.
        5. Actuators.
        6. Piping.

1-14.   Research project.

1-15.   Research project.

1-16.   Research project.

1-17.   Research project.

1-18.   Plant tour.

1-19.   Electrical components such as pressure switches, limit
        switches and relays can be used to operate electrical
        solenoids to control the operation of valves that direct
        fluid to the hydraulic actuators. This permits the design
        of a very versatile fluid power circuit.

1-20.   1. Power brakes.
        2. Power steering.
        3. Shock absorbers.
        4. Air conditioning.
        5. Automotive transmissions.

1-21. A closed-loop system is one which uses feedback whereas an open-loop system does not use feedback.

1-22. 1. Fluid power mechanics.
2. Fluid power technicians.
3. Fluid power engineers.

1-23. Dr. Robert Jarvik made medical history with the design of an artificial, pneumatically actuated heart which sustained the life of Dr. Barney Clark for over 100 days. Two examples are artificial kidneys and valve-assisted bladders.

1-24. The fluid power industry is huge as evidenced by its present annual sales figure of $9.6 billion registered by U.S. Companies and $27.5 billion worldwide. It is also a fast-growing industry with a 48% increase in terms of U.S. equipment sales during the period 1985-1994. The U.S. fluid power industry is larger than many better known industries such as mining machinery, construction equipment and machine tools.

1-25. MPL devices are miniature valve-type devices which by the action of internal moving parts, perform switching operations in fluid logic systems.

1-26. Mechanical displacement, electric voltage, fluid pressure.

1-27. Fluidic devices, which have no moving parts, utilize fluid flow phenomena to perform a wide variety of memory and control functions.

1-28. Fluidic devices must be kept free of contaminants which can obstruct critical air passageways.

1-29. Air has entered the hydraulic oil line and has greatly reduced the Bulk Modulus (measure of stiffness or incompressibility) of the oil-air combination fluid.

1-30. Cruise control is a closed-loop system because the actual automobile highway speed is continuously compared to the operator pre-set input speed via a feedback device. This is why a cruise control system maintains essentially constant speed even when an automobile experiences changing loads while traveling along non-level highways.

1-31. The terms "fluid power" and "hydraulics and pneumatics" are synonymous.

1-32.   Fluid transport systems have as their sole objective the
        delivery of a fluid from one location to another to
        accomplish some useful purpose such as pumping water to
        homes. Fluid power systems are designed specifically to
        perform work such as power steering of automobiles.

1-33.   Changes in oil leakage past seals due to changes in
        viscosity resulting from temperature variations.

1-34.   Hydraulic applications are: automobile power steering and
        brakes, aircraft landing gear, lift trucks and front-end
        loaders.

        Pneumatic applications are: packaging machinery,
        environmental test equipment, artificial heart, logic
        control systems and robotic materials handling devices.

1-35.   Hydraulic brakes. Components are oil lines, oil pumps,
        valves and cylinders.

1-36.   Pneumatically controlled dextrous hand: contains servo-
        controlled pneumatic actuators to give the hand humanlike
        grasping and manipulating capability. Also contains a
        servovalve for precise control of pneumatic actuators to
        provide high speed and force grasping control in
        performing manipulation tasks.

1-37.   Research project.

1-38.   Research project.

1-39.   A PLC is a user-friendly electronic computer designed to
        perform logic functions such as AND, OR and NOT for
        controlling the operation of industrial equipment and
        processes.

1-40.   Unlike general purpose computers, PLCs are designed to
        operate in industrial environments where high ambient
        temperature and humidity levels may exist.

1-41.   Unlike electromechanical relays, PLCs are not hard-wired
        to perform specific functions.

1-42.   1. PLCs are not hard-wired to perform specific functions
           and thus can be readily reprogrammed.
        2. PLCs are more reliable.
        3. PLCs are faster in operation and smaller in size.

1-43.　Developing Biodegradable Fluids: This issue deals with preventing environmental damage caused by potentially harmful material leaking from fluid power systems. Oil companies are developing vegetable based fluids that are biodegradable and compatible with fluid power equipment.

Reducing Oil Leakage: Hydraulic fluid leakage can occur at pipe fittings in hydraulic systems and at mist-lubricators in pneumatic systems. This represents an environmental issue because the EPA has identified oil as a hazardous air pollutant. To resolve this issue, the fluid power industry is striving to produce zero-leakage systems.

Reducing Noise Levels: hydraulic power units such as pumps and motors can operate at noise levels exceeding the limits established by OSHA. New standards of reduced noise levels are being met by fluid power manufacturers in their efforts to produce safe, efficient, reliable, cost effective products.

CHAPTER 2   PROPERTIES OF HYDRAULIC FLUIDS

2-1.   1. Transmit power.
      2. Lubricate moving parts.
      3. Seal clearances between mating parts.

2-2.   1. Good lubricity.
      2. Ideal viscosity
      3. Chemical and environmental stability.
      4. Compatibility with system materials.
      5. Large bulk modulus.
      6. Fire resistance.
      7. Good heat transfer capability.
      8. Low density.
      9. Foam resistance.
    10. Non-toxic.

2-3.   Generally speaking, a fluid should be changed when its
viscosity and acidity increase due to fluid breakdown or
contamination.

2-4.   A liquid is a fluid which, for a given mass, will have a
definite volume independent of the shape of its container.
On the other hand, the volume of a gas will vary to fill
the vessel which contains the gas. Liquids are considered
to be essentially incompressible. Gases, on the other
hand, are fluids which are readily compressible.

2-5.   Advantages of air:
1. Fire resistant.
2. Not messy.

Disadvantages of air:
1. Due to its compressibility, it cannot be used in an
application where accurate positioning or rigid holding
is required.
2. Because it is compressible, it tends to be sluggish.

2-6.   1. Weight density: weight per unit volume.
2. Mass density: mass per unit volume.
3. Specific gravity: the weight density of given fluid
divided by the weight density of water.

2-7.   Pressure is force per unit area.

2-8.   Gage pressures are measured relative to the atmosphere,
whereas absolute pressures are measured relative to a

perfect vacuum such as that which exists in outer space. To distinguish between them, gage pressures are labeled psig or simply psi (Pa gage or kPa gage in Metric units). Absolute pressures are labeled psia (Pa abs or kPa abs in Metric units).

2-9.   Bulk modulus is a measure of the incompressibility of a hydraulic fluid.

2-10.   Viscosity is a measure of the sluggishness with which a fluid flows. Viscosity index is a relative measure of an oil's viscosity change with respect to temperature change.

2-11.   1. High resistance to flow which causes sluggish operation.
        2. Increases power consumption due to frictional losses.

2-12.   1. Increased leakage losses past seals.
        2. Excessive wear due to breakdown of the oil film between moving parts.

2-13.   A Saybolt Universal Second is the viscosity an oil possesses which will allow it to fill a 60-cubic-centimeter container in one second through a standard metering orifice.

2-14.   Pour point is the lowest temperature at which a fluid will flow.

2-15.   Oxidation is caused by the chemical reaction of oxygen from the air with particles of oil. Corrosion is the chemical reaction between a metal and acid.

2-16.   In applications where human safety is of concern.

2-17.   1. Flash point: the temperature at which the oil surface gives off sufficient vapors to ignite when a flame is passed over the surface.
        2. Fire point: the temperature at which the oil will release sufficient vapor to support combustion continuously for 5 seconds when a flame is passed over the surface.
        3. Autogenous ignition temperature: the temperature at which ignition occurs spontaneously.

2-18.   1. Water-glycol solutions.
        2. Water-in-oil emulsions.
        3. Straight systhetics.

14

4. High water content fluids.

2-19. 1. Special paints must be used.
       2. Incompatibility with most natural or synthetic rubber
          seals.
       3. High costs.

2-20. Air can become dissolved or entrained in hydraulic fluids.
       This can cause pump cavitation and also greatly reduce the
       bulk modulus of the hydraulic fluid. Foam resistant fluids
       contain chemical additives which break out entrained air
       to quickly separate the air from the oil while it is in
       the reservoir.

2-21. To prevent wear between the closely fitted working parts.

2-22. Coefficient of friction (CF) is the proportionality
       constant between a normal force (N) and the frictional
       force (F) it creates between two mating surfaces sliding
       relative to each other. (CF = F/N).

2-23. The neutralization number is a measure of the relative
       acidity or alkalinity of a hydraulic fluid and is
       specified by a Ph factor.

2-24. To prevent oxidation.

2-25. It may cause cavitation problems in the pump due to
       excessive vacuum pressure in the pump inlet line unless
       proper design steps are implemented.

2-26. Normally thorough draining, cleaning and flushing are
       required. It may even be necessary to change seals and
       gaskets on the various hydraulic components.

2-27. The height of a column of liquid that represents the
       pressure it develops at its base. For example a 10 foot
       head of oil, having a density of 56 $\frac{lb}{ft^3}$, produces a
       pressure of 0.40 psi at its base.

2-28. By atmospheric pressure at the base of the mercury column.

2-29. As the temperature increases, the viscosity decreases and
       vice versa.

15

2-30.   When the fluid power system operates in an environment
        undergoing large temperature variations such as in outdoor
        machines like automobiles.

2-31.   High viscosity and excessive contamination.

2-32.   Decreases.

2-33.   A high VI should be specified indicating small changes in
        viscosity with respect to changes in temperature.

2-34.   Controlling pollution and conserving natural resources are
        important goals to achieve for the benefit of society.
        Thus it is important to minimize the generation of waste
        hydraulic fluids and to dispose of them in an
        environmentally sound manner.

2-35.   1. Select the optimum fluid for the application involved.
        2. Utilize a well designed filtration system to reduce
           contamination and increase the useful life of the
           fluid.
        3. Follow proper storage procedures of the unused fluid
           supply.
        4. Transporting of the fluids from the storage containers
           to the hydraulic systems, should be done carefully
           since the chances for contamination increase greatly
           with handling.
        5. Operating fluids should be checked regularly for
           viscosity, acidity, bulk modulus, specific gravity,
           water content, color, additive levels, concentration of
           metals and particle contamination.
        6. The entire hydraulic system including pumps, piping,
           fittings, valves, solenoids, filters, actuators and the
           reservoir should be maintained according to
           manufacturer's specifications.
        7. Corrective action should be taken to reduce or
           eliminate leakage from operating hydraulic system.
        8. Disposal of fluids must be done properly. An
           acceptable way to dispose of fluids is to utilize a
           disposal company that is under contract to pick up
           waste hydraulic fluids.

2-36. $$S_g = \frac{\gamma_{fluid}}{\gamma_{water}} = \frac{55\ ^{lb}/_{ft^3}}{62.4\ ^{lb}/_{ft^3}} = \underline{0.881}$$

$$\rho_{fluid} = \frac{\gamma}{g} = \frac{55 \; lb/ft^3}{32.2 \; ft/s^2} = \underline{1.71 \; slugs/ft^3}$$

2-37. $$\gamma \left(\frac{lb}{ft^3}\right) = \frac{372 \; lb}{50 \; gal} \times \frac{1 \; gal}{231 \; in^3} \times \frac{1728 \; in^3}{1 \; ft^3} = \underline{55.7 \; lb/ft^3}$$

2-38. $$\rho \left(kg/m^3\right) = 515 \, \rho \left(slugs/ft^3\right) = 515(1.74) = \underline{896 \; kg/m^3}$$

2-39. $$S_g = \frac{63}{50} = \underline{1.26}$$

2-40. The constant 0.433 is the pressure in psi that is produced at the base of a one-foot column of water. Multiplying this constant by the head of the liquid in feet times the specific gravity of the liquid gives the pressure at the base in units of psi.

2-41. (a) $$S_{g \; air} = \frac{\rho_{air}}{\rho_{water}} = \frac{1.23 \; kg/m^3}{999.1 \; kg/m^3} = \underline{0.00123}$$

(b) $$\frac{S_{g \; water}}{S_{g \; air}} = \frac{1}{0.00123} = \underline{813}$$

2-42. $$\text{Volume} = A_{base} \times h = \frac{\pi}{4}\left(0.5 \; m\right)^2 \times 1 \; m = 0.196 \; m^3$$

$$\text{Weight} = \gamma V = 2000 \; N/m^3 \times 0.196 \; m^3 = 392 \; N$$

$$M = \frac{W}{g} = \frac{392 \; N}{9.81 \; m/s^2} = \underline{40.0 \; kg}$$

2-43. (a) $$\gamma = \frac{W}{V} = \frac{8.70 \; N}{0.001 \; m^3} = \underline{8700 \; N/m^3}$$

(b) $$\rho = \frac{\gamma}{g} = \frac{8700 \; N/m^3}{9.81 \; m/s^2} = \underline{888 \; kg/m^3}$$

(c) $S_{g\,oil} = \dfrac{\rho_{oil}}{\rho_{water}} = \dfrac{888}{999} = \underline{0.889}$

2-44. $P = 0.433\,H\,S_g = 0.433 \times 30 \times 0.881 = \underline{11.4\ \text{psi}}$

2-45. $P_{abs} = (26.0 + 14.7)\ \text{psi} \times \dfrac{1}{0.000145\ \frac{psi}{Pa}} = 280{,}700\ \text{Pa abs}$

$= \underline{280.7\ \text{kPa abs}}$

2-46. $-2\ \text{kPa} + 101\ \text{kPa} = \underline{99\ \text{kPa abs}}$

2-47. $V = A_{base} \times h$

$V(ft^3) = 2\,\text{ft} \times 2\,\text{ft} \times h(ft) = 4\,h(ft)$

$V(ft^3) = V(gal) \times \dfrac{231\ in^3}{1\ gal} \times \dfrac{1\ ft^3}{1728\ in^3} = 0.134\,V(gal)$

Hence we have: $0.134\ V(gal) = 4\ h(ft)$

Or $h(ft) = \dfrac{0.134\ V(gal)}{4} = \dfrac{0.134 \times 100}{4} = \underline{3.35\ \text{ft}}$

2-48. $P(psi) = 0.433\ H(ft) \times S_g = 0.433 \times 100 \sin 30^\circ \times 0.9 = \underline{19.5\ \text{psi}}$

2-49. $P = \dfrac{F}{A} = \dfrac{13{,}300\ N}{\dfrac{\pi}{4}(0.250\ m)^2} = \dfrac{13{,}300\ N}{0.0491\ m^2} = 271{,}000\ \text{Pa gage}$

$= \underline{271\ \text{kPa gage}}$

2-50. $P = \text{cons}\tan t = \dfrac{F}{A}$

$\dfrac{F}{500} = \dfrac{100}{50}$ Hence $F = \underline{1000\ N}$

2-51. $V_{small\ piston} = V_{large\ piston}$

$\left(A\,S\right)_{small\ piston} = \left(A\,S\right)_{large\ piston}$

$$(50 \times 10) = \left(500\,S\right) \qquad \text{Hence} \quad S = \underline{1\ \text{cm}}$$

2-52. $\Delta\,P\!\left(psi\right) = 0.433\ \Delta\ H(ft) \times S_g \qquad \text{Assu min g } S_g = 0.9\,,\ \text{we have:}$

$$\Delta\,P\!\left(psi\right) = 0.433 \times 20 \times 0.9 = 7.79\ psi$$

$$\text{Thus} \quad F_{\tan k\ top} = 15 - 7.79 = 7.21\ psi$$

$$F = P\,A = 7.21\,\frac{lb}{in^2} \times \frac{\pi}{4}\left(10 \times 12\ \text{in.}\right)^2 = \underline{81{,}500\ lb}$$

Pascal's Law states that pressure in a static body of fluid is transmitted equally only at the same elevation level. Pressure increases with depth and vice versa in accordance with the following equation:

$$\Delta\,P = 0.433\left(\Delta\ H\right)S_g$$

Changes in pressure due to elevation changes can be ignored in a fluid power system as long as they are small compared to the magnitude of the system pressure produced at the pump discharge port. For example a pump discharge pressure of 1000 psi becomes 996 psi at an elevation 10 ft above the pump. This is only a 0.4% drop in pressure.

2-53. $P = cons\tan t = \dfrac{F}{A}$

$$\frac{F}{\dfrac{\pi}{4}\,(6)^2} = \frac{100}{\dfrac{\pi}{4}\,(2)^2} \qquad \text{Hence} \quad F = \underline{900\ lb}$$

2-54. $V_{small\ piston} = V_{l\,arg\,e\ piston}$

$$\left(A\ S\right)_{small\ piston} = \left(A\ S\right)_{l\,arg\,e\ piston}$$

$$\frac{\pi}{4}\,(2)^2 \times 1.5 = \frac{\pi}{4}\,(6)^2\ S \qquad \text{Hence} \quad S = \underline{0.167\ \text{in.}}$$

2-55. $P_{piston} = P_{air} - \gamma_{oil}\ H_{oil}$

$$= 550{,}000 \text{ Pa} - \left(0.90 \times 9797 \frac{N}{m^3}\right) \times 1 \text{ m}$$

$$= 550{,}000 \text{ Pa} - 8820 \text{ Pa} = 541{,}180 \text{ Pa}$$

$$W = P A = 541{,}180 \times \frac{\pi}{4} (0.250)^2 = \underline{26{,}565 \text{ N}}$$

Ignoring the 1 m head of oil, the maximum weight automobile that can be lifted is:

$$W = P A = 550{,}000 \times \frac{\pi}{4} (0.250)^2 = 26{,}998 \text{ N}$$

$$\% \text{ Error} = \frac{26{,}998 - 26{,}565}{26{,}565} \times 100 = \underline{1.63 \%}$$

2-56. $\quad \left(\Delta v\right) = \dfrac{- v\left(\Delta P\right)}{\beta} = \dfrac{- 20\,(950)}{300{,}000} = \underline{- 0.0633 \text{ in}^3}$

2-57. $\quad \dfrac{\Delta V}{V} = \dfrac{- \Delta P}{\beta} = \dfrac{- 49 \times 101}{1{,}750{,}000} = -0.00283 = \underline{- 0.283 \%}$

2-58. $\quad \beta = \dfrac{v\left(\Delta P\right)}{\Delta V}$

Where $\quad \Delta V = \dfrac{\pi d^2}{4} L = \dfrac{\pi (2)^2}{4} \times 0.01 = 0.0314 \text{ in}^3$

And $\quad \Delta P = \dfrac{\Delta F}{A} = \dfrac{5000}{\dfrac{\pi}{4} (2)^2} = 1592 \text{ psi}$

Thus $\quad \beta = \dfrac{10\,(1592)}{0.0314} = \underline{507{,}000 \text{ psi}}$

2-59. $\quad \beta = \dfrac{v\left(\Delta P\right)}{\Delta V} \qquad \text{where}$

$$V = 10 \text{ in}^3 \times \left(\frac{1 \text{ m}}{39.4 \text{ in.}}\right)^3 = 163 \times 10^{-6} \text{ m}^3$$

$$\Delta V = 0.0314 \text{ in}^3 \times \left(\frac{1 \text{ m}}{39.4 \text{ in.}}\right)^3 = 0.513 \times 10^{-6} \text{ m}^3$$

$$\Delta P = 1592 \text{ psi} \times \frac{1 \text{ Pa}}{0.000145 \text{ psi}} = 10.98 \times 10^6 \text{ Pa}$$

$$\text{Thus } \beta = 163 \times 10^{-6} \times \frac{10.98 \times 10^6}{0.513 \times 10^{-6}} = 3489 \times 10^6 \text{ Pa} = \underline{3489 \text{ MPa}}$$

2-60. $\quad v \text{ (cS)} = 0.220 \, t - \dfrac{135}{t} = 0.220 \times 200 - \dfrac{135}{200} = \underline{43.3 \text{ cS}}$

$\quad\quad \mu \text{ (cP)} = 0.9 \times v \text{ (cS)} = 0.9 \times 43.3 = \underline{39.0 \text{ cP}}$

2-61. $\quad VI = \dfrac{L - U}{L - H} \times 100$

$\quad\quad 70 = \dfrac{375 - U}{375 - 125} \times 100 \quad\quad \text{Thus } U = \underline{200 \text{ SUS}}$

2-62. $\quad \text{(CF)} = 2.83 \dfrac{F \times r}{L \times s} = 2.83 \dfrac{50 \times 7.75}{20,000 \times 1.40} = \underline{0.0392}$

2-63. $\quad \mu\left(\dfrac{N \bullet s}{m^2}\right) = \mu\left(\dfrac{lb - s}{ft^2}\right) \times \dfrac{4.448 \text{ N}}{1 \text{ lb}} \times \left(\dfrac{1 \text{ ft}}{0.3048 \text{ m}}\right)^2$

$\quad\quad \text{Therefore } 1 \dfrac{lb - s}{ft^2} = \underline{47.88 \dfrac{N \bullet s}{m^2}}$

2-64. $\quad v\left(\dfrac{m^2}{s}\right) = v\left(\dfrac{ft^2}{s}\right) \times \left(\dfrac{0.3048 \text{ m}}{1 \text{ ft}}\right)^2$

$\quad\quad \text{Therefore } 1 \dfrac{ft^2}{s} = \underline{0.0929 \dfrac{m^2}{s}}$

2-65. $\quad v \text{ (cS)} = \dfrac{\mu \text{ (cP)}}{S_g} = \dfrac{1200}{0.89} = 1348 \text{ cS} = 13.48 \text{ Stokes} = \underline{13.48 \dfrac{cm^2}{s}}$

$$\nu \left(\frac{ft^2}{s} \right) = \nu \left(\frac{cm^2}{s} \right) \times \left(\frac{1 \ in.}{2.54 \ cm} \right) \times \left(\frac{1 \ ft}{12 \ in.} \right)^2$$

$$= 13.48 \times \left(\frac{1}{2.54} \right)^2 \times \left(\frac{1}{12} \right)^2 = 0.0145 \frac{ft^2}{s}$$

CHAPTER 3   ENERGY AND POWER IN HYDRAULIC SYSTEMS

3-1.   The total energy at upstream station 1 in a pipeline plus the energy added by a pump minus the energy removed by a motor minus the energy loss due to friction, equals the total energy at downstream station 2. If a section of horizontal pipe contains no pump or motor, the pressure at a small diameter location will be less than the pressure at a large diameter location. Pressure energy is transformed into kinetic energy in the small diameter location.

3-2.   The weight flow rate is the same for all cross-sections of a pipe. Thus the smaller the pipe diameter, the greater the velocity and vice versa.

3-3.   Ideally the velocity of a free jet of fluid is equal to the square root of the product of two times the acceleration of gravity times the head producing the jet.

3-4.   As shown in Figure 3-19, in order for a siphon to work, the following two conditions must be met:

1. The elevation of the free end must be lower than the elevation of the liquid surface inside the container.

2. The fluid must be initially forced to flow up from the container into the center portion of the U-tube. This is normally done by temporarily providing a suction pressure at the free end of the siphon.

3-5.   Energy can neither be created nor destroyed.

3-6.   Per Figure 3-16, the volume of air flow is determined by the opening position of the butterfly valve. As the air flows through the venturi, it speeds up and loses some of its pressure. This produces a differential pressure between the fuel bowl and the venturi throat. This causes gasoline to flow into the air stream.

3-7.   Using Figure 3-14 as a reference we have:

Z is called "elevation head" or elevation energy per lb of fluid.

$\dfrac{P}{\gamma}$ is called "pressure head" or pressure energy per lb of fluid.

$\dfrac{v^2}{2g}$ is called "velocity head" or kinetic energy per lb of fluid.

3-8.   1. A force is required to change the motion of a body.
        2. If a body is acted upon by a force, the body will have an acceleration proportional to the magnitude of the force and inversely to the mass of the body.
        3. If one body exerts a force on a second body, the second body must exert an equal but opposite force on the first body.

3-9.   Energy is the ability to perform work. Power is the rate of doing work.

3-10.   Torque equals the product of a force and moment arm which is measured from the center of a shaft (center of rotation) perpendicularly to the line of action of the force.

3-11.   Efficiency, another significant parameter when dealing with work and power, is defined as output power divided by input power.

3-12.   Mechanical power equals force times velocity.
        Electrical power equals volts times amps.
        Hydraulic power(or fluid power) equals pressure times flow rate.

3-13.   Elevation head is potential energy per unit weight of fluid.
        Pressure head is pressure energy per unit weight of fluid.
        Velocity head is kinetic energy per unit weight of fluid.

3-14.   (a) First find the force acting on the rod of the pump.

$$F_{rod} = \frac{8}{2} \times F_{input} = \frac{8}{2} \times 20 = 80 \text{ lb}$$

Next calculate the pump discharge pressure P.

$$P = \frac{\text{rod force}}{\text{piston area}} = \frac{F_{red}}{A_{pump\ piston}} = \frac{80\ lb}{\frac{\pi}{4}(2)^2\ in^2} = 25.5\ psi$$

We can now calculate the load-carrying capacity.

$$F_{load} = P\ A_{load\ piston} = \left(25.5\ \frac{lb}{in^2}\right) \times \frac{\pi}{4}(4)^2\ in^2 = \underline{320.4\ lb}$$

(b) Total volume of oil ejected from the pump equals the volume of oil displacing the load cylinder.

$$(A \times S)_{pump\ piston} \times (\text{no. of cycles}) = (A \times S)_{load\ piston}$$

$$\frac{\pi}{4}(2)^2\ in^2 \times 3\ in \times 20 = \frac{\pi}{4}(4)^2\ in^2 \times S_{load\ piston}(in)$$

Thus $S_{load\ piston} = \underline{15\ in.}$

(c) $\text{Power} = \frac{F \times s}{t} = \frac{320.4\ lb \times \frac{15}{12}\ ft}{15\ s} = 26.7\ \frac{ft-lb}{s}$

$$HP_{100\%\ efficiency} = \frac{26.7}{550} = 0.0485\ HP$$

$$HP_{90\%\ efficiency} = 0.90 \times 0.0485 = \underline{0.0437\ HP}$$

3-15. Metric data are:

$$\text{Pump piston diameter} = 2\ in \times \frac{2.54\ cm}{1\ in} = 5.08\ cm$$

$$\text{Load cylinder diameter} = 4\ in \times \frac{2.54\ cm}{1\ in} = 10.16\ cm$$

$$\text{Average hand force} = 20\ lb \times \frac{1\ N}{0.225\ lb} = 88.9\ N$$

$$\text{Pump piston stroke} = 3\ in \times \frac{2.54\ cm}{1\ in} = 7.62\ cm$$

(a) First find the force acting on the rod of the pump.

$$F_{rod} = \frac{8}{2} \times F_{input} = \frac{8}{2} \times 88.9 \text{ N} = 355.6 \text{ N}$$

Next calculate the pump discharge pressure P.

$$P = \frac{\text{rod force}}{\text{piston area}} = \frac{F_{rod}}{A_{pump\ piston}} = \frac{355.6 \text{ N}}{\frac{\pi}{4}\left(0.0508 \text{ m}\right)^2} = 175,000 \text{ Pa}$$

We can now calculate the load carrying capacity.

$$F_{load} = P \times A_{load\ piston} = 175,000 \frac{\text{N}}{\text{m}^2} \times \frac{\pi}{4}\left(0.1016 \text{ m}\right)^2 = \underline{1419 \text{ N}}$$

(b) Total volume of oil ejected from the pump equals the volume of oil displacing the load cylinder.

$$(A \times S)_{pump\ piston} \times \left(\text{no. of cycles}\right) = (A \times S)_{load\ piston}$$

$$\frac{\pi}{4}(0.0508)^2 \text{ m}^2 \times 0.0762 \text{ m} \times 20 = \frac{\pi}{4}(0.1016)^2 \text{ m}^2 \times S_{load\ piston}$$

$$S_{load\ piston} = 0.381 \text{ m} = \underline{38.1 \text{ cm}}$$

(c) Power $= \dfrac{F \times S}{t} = \dfrac{1419 \text{ N} \times 0.381 \text{ m}}{15 \text{ s}} = 36.0 \dfrac{\text{N} \bullet \text{m}}{\text{s}} = \underline{36.0 \text{ Watts}}$

Power (@ 90% efficiency) $= 0.90 \times 36.0 = \underline{32.4 \text{ Watts}}$

3-16.   First find the booster discharge pressure P_2.

$$P_2 = \frac{P_1 \times A_1}{A_2} = \frac{125 \times 20}{1} = 2500 \text{ psi}$$

Per Pascal's Law, $P_3 = P_2 = 2500 \text{ psi}$

$$A_3 = \frac{F}{P_3} = \frac{75,000 \text{ lb}}{2500 \text{ lb}/\text{in}^2} = \underline{30 \text{ in}^2}$$

3-17.   Metric data are:

$$P_1 = 125 \text{ psi} \times \frac{101,000 \text{ Pa}}{14.7 \text{ psi}} = 859,000 \text{ Pa}$$

$$A_1 = 20 \text{ in}^2 \times \left(\frac{2.54 \text{ cm}}{1 \text{ in.}}\right)^2 = 129 \text{ cm}^2$$

$$A_2 = 1 \text{ in}^2 \times \left(\frac{2.54 \text{ cm}}{1 \text{ in}}\right)^2 = 6.45 \text{ cm}^2$$

$$F = 75{,}000 \text{ lb} \times \frac{1 \text{ N}}{0.225 \text{ lb}} = 333{,}000 \text{ N}$$

$$P_2 = \frac{P_1 A_1}{A_2} = \frac{859{,}000 \text{ Pa} \times 129 \text{ cm}^2}{6.45 \text{ cm}^2} = 17{,}180{,}000 \text{ Pa} = 17.18 \text{ MPa}$$

$$P_3 = P_2 = 17.18 \text{ MPa}$$

$$A_3 = \frac{F}{P_3} = \frac{333{,}000 \text{ N}}{17.18 \times 10^6 \text{ N}/{\text{m}^2}} = \underline{0.0194 \text{ m}^2}$$

3-18.
$$P_2 = \frac{P_1 A_1}{A_2} = \frac{1 \text{ MPa} \times 0.02 \text{ m}^2}{0.001 \text{ m}^2} = 20 \text{ MPa}$$

$$P_3 = P_2 = 20 \text{ MPa}$$

$$A_3 = \frac{F}{P_3} = \frac{300{,}000 \text{ N}}{20 \times 10^6 \text{ N}/{\text{m}^2}} = \underline{0.015 \text{ m}^2}$$

3-19.
$$H = \frac{P(\text{psi})}{0.433 \, S_g} = \frac{5}{0.433 \times 0.90} = \underline{12.8 \text{ ft}}$$

3-20.
$$P = -0.433 \, H(\text{ft}) \, S_g = -0.433 \times 4 \times 0.9 = \underline{-1.56 \text{ psig}}$$

Frictional losses and changes in kinetic energy would cause the pressure at the pump inlet to increase negatively (greater suction pressure) because pressure energy decreases per Bernoulli's Equation. This would increase the chances for having pump cavitation because the pump inlet pressure more closely approaches the vapor pressure of the fluid (usually about 5 psi suction or -5 psig) allowing for the formation and collapse of vapor bubbles.

3-21. $P = \dfrac{F_1}{A_1} = \dfrac{2000}{\dfrac{\pi}{4}(3)^2} = 283 \text{ psi}$

$F_2 = P \times A_2 = 283 \times \dfrac{\pi}{4}(1)^2 = 222 \text{ lb}$

$F(16) = 222(1) \quad \text{so} \quad F = \underline{23.9 \text{ lb}}$

$A_1 S_1 = A_2 S_2 \quad \text{so} \quad S_1 = \dfrac{A_2}{A_1} \times S_2 = \left(\dfrac{1}{3}\right)^2 \times \dfrac{5}{16} = \underline{0.0347 \text{ in.}}$

3-22. $F_1 = 2000 \text{ lb} \times \dfrac{1 \text{ N}}{0.225 \text{ lb}} = 8890 \text{ N}$

$A_1 = \dfrac{\pi}{4}(3 \text{ in.})^2 \times \left(\dfrac{1 \text{ m}}{39.4 \text{ in.}}\right)^2 = 0.00455 \text{ m}^2$

$P = \dfrac{F_1}{A_1} = \dfrac{8890 \text{ N}}{0.00455 \text{ m}^2} = 1.95 \text{ MPa}$

$F_2 = P A_2 \quad \text{where} \quad A_2 = \dfrac{\pi}{4}(1 \text{ in})^2 \times \left(\dfrac{1 \text{ m}}{39.4 \text{ in}}\right)^2 = 0.000506 \text{ m}^2$

$F_2 = \left(1.95 \times 10^6\right) \times \left(506 \times 10^{-6}\right) = 987 \text{ N}$

$F = 987 \times \dfrac{1}{16} = \underline{61.7 \text{ N}}$

$A_1 S_1 = A_2 S_2 \quad \text{where} \quad S_2 = \dfrac{5}{16} \text{ in} \times \dfrac{1 \text{ m}}{39.4 \text{ in}} = 0.00793 \text{ m}$

$S_1 = \dfrac{A_2}{A_1} \times S_2 = \dfrac{1}{9} \times 0.793 \text{ cm} = \underline{0.0881 \text{ cm}}$

3-23. $Q = \dfrac{v D^2}{0.408} = \dfrac{10 (1)^2}{0.408} = \underline{24.5 \text{ gpm}}$

3-24. $D = \sqrt{\dfrac{0.408 Q}{v}} = \sqrt{\dfrac{0.408 \times 20}{15}} = \underline{0.738 \text{ in.}}$

3-25. Metric data are:

$$\text{Velocity} = 15\ \frac{\text{ft}}{\text{s}} \times \frac{1\ \text{m}}{3.28\ \text{ft}} = 4.57\ \frac{\text{m}}{\text{s}}$$

$$\text{Flow rate}\left(\frac{\text{m}^3}{\text{s}}\right) = 0.0000632\ Q(\text{gpm})$$

$$= 0.0000632 \times 20 = 0.001264\ \frac{\text{m}^3}{\text{s}}$$

$$\frac{\pi}{4} D^2 = A = \frac{Q}{v} = \frac{0.001264\ \frac{\text{m}^3}{\text{s}}}{4.57\ \frac{\text{m}}{\text{s}}} = 0.0002766\ \text{m}^2$$

$$D = \sqrt{\frac{4 \times 0.0002766}{\pi}} = \underline{0.0188\ \text{m}}$$

3-26.
$$v\left(\frac{\text{m}}{\text{s}}\right) = \frac{Q\left(\frac{\text{m}^3}{\text{s}}\right)}{A\left(\text{m}^2\right)} = \frac{Q\left(\frac{\text{m}^3}{\text{s}}\right)}{\frac{\pi}{4}\left[D\ (\text{m})\right]^2} = \frac{C\,Q\left(\frac{\text{m}^3}{\text{s}}\right)}{\left[D\ (\text{m})\right]^2}$$

$$\text{Therefore } C = \frac{4}{\pi} = \underline{1.273}$$

$$v\left(\frac{\text{m}}{\text{s}}\right) = \frac{1.273 \times 0.001896}{(0.0254)^2} = \underline{3.74\ \frac{\text{m}}{\text{s}}}$$

Velocity value agrees with that of Example 3-11.

3-27.
$$Q\left(\frac{\text{m}^3}{\text{s}}\right) = A\left(\text{m}^2\right) \times v\left(\frac{\text{m}}{\text{s}}\right) = \frac{\pi}{4}\,(0.10)^2 \times 3 = \underline{0.0236\ \frac{\text{m}^3}{\text{s}}}$$

3-28.
$$v = \frac{0.408\,Q}{D^2} = \frac{0.408 \times 20}{4^2} = 0.51\ \frac{\text{ft}}{\text{s}}$$

$$t = \frac{L}{v} = \frac{\left(\frac{20}{12}\right)\text{ft}}{0.51\ \frac{\text{ft}}{\text{s}}} = \underline{3.27\ \text{s}}$$

3-29.
$$v = \frac{Q}{A} = \frac{20\ \frac{\text{gal}}{\text{min}} \times \frac{231\ \text{in}^3}{1\ \text{gal}} \times \frac{1\ \text{min}}{60\ \text{s}}}{\frac{\pi}{4}\left(4^2 - 2^2\right)\text{in}^2} = \frac{77\ \frac{\text{in}^3}{\text{s}}}{9.42\ \text{in}^2} = 8.17\ \frac{\text{in}}{\text{s}}$$

$$t = \frac{L}{v} = \frac{20 \text{ in.}}{8.17 \text{ in}/_s} = \underline{2.45 \text{ s}}$$

3-30. $$V/_{min} = A \, L \, N = \frac{\pi}{4}(3^2 - 2^2)\text{in}^2 \times (2 \times 20)\text{in} \times \frac{60}{\text{min}} = 4710 \text{ in}^3/_{min}$$

$$Q = V/_{min} = 4710 \frac{\text{in}^3}{\text{min}} \times \frac{1 \text{ gal}}{231 \text{ in}^3} = \underline{20.4 \text{ gpm}}$$

3-31. $$Q_{pipe} = 10 \text{ gpm} \times \frac{\frac{\pi}{4}(3)^2}{\frac{\pi}{4}(3^2 - 1.5^2)} = \underline{13.3 \text{ gpm}}$$

$$ID_{pipe}\left(\text{per Figure } 4-1\right) = 0.824 \text{ in.}$$

$$v = \frac{Q}{A} = \frac{10 \frac{\text{gal}}{\text{min}} \times \frac{231 \text{ in}^3}{1 \text{ gal}} \times \frac{1 \text{ min}}{60 \text{ s}}}{\frac{\pi}{4}\left(0.824 \text{ in}\right)^2} = 72.2 \text{ in}/_s = \underline{6.02 \text{ ft}/_s}$$

3-32. $Q = ALN$ Substituting values we have:

$$0.030 \frac{\text{m}^3}{\text{min}} = \frac{\pi}{4}(0.08)^2 \text{ m}^2 \times 0.35 \text{ m} \times N\left(\frac{\text{cycles}}{\text{min}}\right)$$
$$+ \frac{\pi}{4}\left(0.08^2 - 0.03^2\right) \text{ m}^2 \times 0.35 \text{ m} \times N\left(\frac{\text{cycles}}{\text{min}}\right)$$
$$0.030 = (0.00176 + 0.00151) \times N \quad \text{so} \quad N = \underline{9.2} \frac{\text{cycles}}{\text{min}}$$

3-33. $$Q_1 = A_1 v_1 = \frac{\pi}{4}\left(0.10 \text{ m}\right)^2 \times 5 \text{ m}/_s = 0.0393 \text{ m}^3/_s$$

$$Q_2 = Q_3 = \frac{Q_1}{2} = 0.0197 \frac{\text{m}^3}{\text{s}}$$

$$v_2 = \frac{Q_2}{A_2} = \frac{0.0197 \text{ m}^3/_s}{\frac{\pi}{4}(0.07)^2 \text{ m}^2} = \underline{5.12 \text{ m}/_s}$$

$$v_3 = \frac{Q_3}{A_3} = \frac{0.0197 \ m^3/s}{\frac{\pi}{4}(0.06)^2 \ m^2} = \underline{6.97 \ m/s}$$

3-34. $HP = \frac{P(psi) \times Q(gpm)}{1714}$ Substituting values we have:

$$5 = \frac{1000 \times Q(gpm)}{1714}$$ Hence $Q = 8.57 \ gpm$

3-35.   (a) $A = \frac{F_{load}}{P} = \frac{10,000 \ lb}{1,000 \ lb/in^2} = \underline{10 \ in^2}$

(b) $Q\left(\frac{ft^3}{s}\right) = \frac{A(ft^2) \times S(ft)}{t(s)} = \frac{\frac{10}{144} \times 8}{8} = \underline{0.0694 \ \frac{ft^3}{s}}$

$Q(gpm) = 448 \ Q\left(\frac{ft^3}{s}\right) = 448 \times 0.0694 = \underline{31.1 \ gpm}$

(c) $HP = \frac{1000 \times 31.1}{1714} = \underline{18.1 \ HP}$

3-36. $H_p(m) = \frac{Pump \ Power \ (W)}{\gamma\left(N/m^3\right) \times Q\left(m^3/s\right)}$ where $\gamma = \gamma_{water} \times S_g = 9797 \ S_g$

Thus $H_p(m) = \frac{1000 \times Pump \ Power \ (kW)}{9797 \ S_g \times Q\left(m^3/s\right)} = \frac{0.1021 \ Pump \ Power(kW)}{Q\left(m^3/s\right) \times S_g}$

3-37. $HP = \frac{F(lb) \times v\left(ft/s\right)}{550}$

Therefore $v = \frac{550 \times HP}{F(lb)} = \frac{550 \times 10}{5000} = \underline{1.1 \ ft/s}$

3-38. $Power(kW) = F(kN) \times v\left(m/s\right)$

Thus $\quad v\left(\frac{m}{s}\right) = \dfrac{\text{Power(kW)}}{\text{F(kN)}} = \dfrac{10}{20} = \underline{0.5 \; \frac{m}{s}}$

3-39. $\quad \text{Flowrate}\left(\frac{m^3}{s}\right) = \dfrac{\text{Power(kW)}}{\text{Pressure(kPa)}} = \dfrac{5}{10,000} = \underline{0.0005 \; \frac{m^3}{s}}$

3-40. (a) $A = \dfrac{F}{P} = \dfrac{40,000 \text{ N}}{10 \times 10^6 \; \frac{N}{m^2}} = \underline{0.004 \text{ m}^2}$

(b) $Q = A\,v = 0.004 \text{ m}^2 \times \dfrac{3 \text{ m}}{8 \text{ s}} = \underline{0.0015 \; \frac{m^3}{s}}$

(c) $\text{Power} = PQ = \left(10 \times 10^3 \text{ kPa}\right) \times \left(0.0015 \; \frac{m^3}{s}\right) = \underline{15 \text{ kW}}$

3-41. (a) $W = FL = 3500 \text{ lb} \times 7 \text{ ft} = \underline{24,500 \text{ ft} \cdot \text{lb}}$

(b) $P = \dfrac{F}{A} = \dfrac{3500 \text{ lb}}{\frac{\pi}{4}(8)^2 \text{ in}^2} = \underline{69.7 \text{ psi}}$

(c) $\text{Power} = \dfrac{24,500 \text{ ft} \cdot \text{lb}}{10 \text{ s}} = 2450 \; \dfrac{\text{ft} \cdot \text{lb}}{s} = \dfrac{2450}{550} \text{ HP} = \underline{4.45 \text{ HP}}$

(d) $v = \dfrac{Q}{A} = \dfrac{10 \; \frac{\text{gal}}{\text{min}} \times \frac{231 \text{ in}^3}{1 \text{ gal}} \times \frac{1 \text{ min}}{60 \text{ s}}}{\frac{\pi}{4}\left(8^2 - 4^2\right) \text{ in}^2} = \underline{1.02 \; \frac{in}{s}}$

(e) $Q = A\,v = \dfrac{\pi}{4}\left(8^2 - 4^2\right) \text{in}^2 \times \dfrac{7 \times 12 \text{ in}}{10 \text{ s}} \times \dfrac{1 \text{ gal}}{231 \text{ in}^3} \times \dfrac{60 \text{ s}}{1 \text{ min}}$

$= \underline{82.2 \text{ gpm}}$

3-42. (a) $F = 3500 \text{ lb} \times \dfrac{1 \text{ N}}{0.225 \text{ lb}} = \underline{15,600 \text{ N}}$

$L = 7 \text{ ft} \times \dfrac{1 \text{ m}}{3.28 \text{ ft}} = 2.13 \text{ m}$

$W = FL = 15,600 \text{ N} \times 2.13 \text{ m} = \underline{33,200 \text{ N} \cdot \text{m}}$

(b) $A = \frac{\pi}{4}(8)^2 \text{ in}^2 = 50.2 \text{ in}^2 = 50.2 \text{ in}^2 \times \left(\frac{1 \text{ m}}{39.4 \text{ in.}}\right)^2 = 0.0324 \text{ m}^2$

$P = \frac{F}{A} = \frac{15{,}600 \text{ N}}{0.0324 \text{ m}^2} = 481{,}000 \text{ N}/\text{m}^2 = \underline{481 \text{ kPa}}$

(c) $\text{Power} = \frac{33{,}200 \text{ N} \cdot \text{m}}{10 \text{ s}} = 3320 \frac{\text{N} \cdot \text{m}}{\text{s}} = 3320 \text{ W} = \underline{3.32 \text{ kW}}$

(d) $Q = 10 \frac{\text{gal}}{\text{min}} \times \frac{231 \text{ in}^3}{1 \text{ gal}} \times \left(\frac{1 \text{ m}}{39.4 \text{ in}}\right)^3 \times \frac{1 \text{ min}}{60 \text{ s}} = 0.000629 \text{ m}^3/\text{s}$

$v = \frac{Q}{A} = \frac{0.000629 \text{ m}^3/\text{s}}{\frac{\pi}{4}\left(8^2 - 4^2\right)\text{in}^2 \times \left(\frac{1 \text{ m}}{39.4 \text{ in}}\right)^2} = \frac{0.000629 \text{ m}^3/\text{s}}{0.0243 \text{ m}^2}$

$= \underline{0.0259 \text{ m/s}}$

(e) $Q = A\,v = 0.0243 \text{ m}^2 \times \left(\frac{2.13 \text{ m}}{10 \text{ s}}\right) = \underline{0.00518 \text{ m}^3/\text{s}}$

3-43. $Z_1 + \frac{P_1}{\gamma} + \frac{v_1^2}{2g} = Z_2 + \frac{P_2}{\gamma} + \frac{v_2^2}{2g}$

$v_1 = \frac{0.408 \, Q}{D_1^2} = \frac{0.408 \times 100}{2^2} = 10.2 \frac{\text{ft}}{\text{s}}$

$v_2 = \frac{0.408 \times 100}{1^2} = 40.8 \frac{\text{ft}}{\text{s}}$

$\frac{P_1 - P_2}{\gamma} = \frac{v_2^2 - v_1^2}{2g} = \frac{40.8^2 - 10.2^2}{64.4} = \frac{1665 - 104}{64.4} = 24.2 \text{ ft}$

$P_1 - P_2 = 24.2 \times 62.4 \times 0.9 = 1359 \text{ lb}/\text{ft}^2 = 9.4 \text{ psi}$

$P_2 = P_1 - 9.4 = 10 - 9.4 = \underline{0.6 \text{ psig}}$

3-44. $Z_1 + \frac{P_1}{\gamma} + \frac{v_1^2}{2g} = Z_2 + \frac{P_2}{\gamma} + \frac{v_2^2}{2g}$

$$P_1 = 10 \text{ psi} \times \frac{1 \text{ Pa}}{0.000145 \text{ psi}} = 69{,}000 \text{ Pa}$$

$$Q\left(\frac{m^3}{s}\right) = 0.0000632 \, Q(\text{gpm}) = 0.0000632 \times 100 = 0.00632 \frac{m^2}{s}$$

$$D_1 = 2 \text{ in} \times \frac{1 \text{ ft}}{12 \text{ in}} \times \frac{1 \text{ m}}{3.28 \text{ ft}} = 0.0508 \text{ m} \quad \text{Thus } D_2 = 0.0254 \text{ m}$$

$$v_1 = \frac{Q}{A_1} = \frac{0.00632 \frac{m^3}{s}}{\frac{\pi}{4}(0.0508)^2 \ m^2} = 3.12 \frac{m}{s}$$

$$v_2 = \frac{Q}{A_2} = \frac{0.00632}{\frac{\pi}{4}(0.0254)^2} = 12.4 \frac{m}{s}$$

$$\frac{P_1 - P_2}{\gamma} = \frac{v_2^2 - v_1^2}{2g} = \frac{12.4^2 - 3.12^2}{2 \times 9.81} = \frac{153.8 - 9.7}{2 \times 9.81} = 7.34 \text{ m}$$

$$P_1 - P_2 = 7.34 \times 9800 \times 0.9 = 64{,}700 \text{ Pa}$$

$$P_2 = P_1 - 64{,}700 = 69{,}000 - 64{,}700 = \underline{4300 \ \textbf{Pa gage}}$$

3-45.
$$W Z = 1000 \text{ gal} \times \frac{231 \text{ in}^3}{1 \text{ gal}} \times \frac{1 \text{ ft}^3}{1728 \text{ in}^3} \times 62.4 \frac{\text{lb}}{\text{ft}^3} \times 100 \text{ ft}$$

$$= \underline{834{,}000 \ \textbf{ft} \bullet \textbf{lb}}$$

3-46.
$$\frac{W v^2}{2g} = 1 \text{ gal} \times \frac{231 \text{ in}^3}{1 \text{ gal}} \times \frac{1 \text{ ft}^3}{1728 \text{ in}^3} \times 62.4 \frac{\text{lb}}{\text{ft}^3} \times \left(20 \frac{\text{ft}}{\text{s}}\right)^2 \times \frac{1}{64.4 \frac{\text{ft}}{\text{s}^2}}$$

$$= \underline{51.8 \ \textbf{ft} \bullet \textbf{lb}}$$

3-47.
$$v_2 = \sqrt{2gh} = \sqrt{64.4 \times 25} = 40.1 \frac{\text{ft}}{\text{s}}$$

$$Q = \frac{v D^2}{0.408} = \frac{40 \times 1^2}{0.408} = \underline{98.3 \ \textbf{gpm}}$$

3-48.
$$v_2 = \sqrt{2gh} \quad \text{where} \quad h = 25 \text{ ft} \times \frac{1 \text{ m}}{3.28 \text{ ft}} = 7.62 \text{ m}$$

Thus $v_2 = \sqrt{2 \times 9.81 \times 7.62} = 12.2 \,^m/_s$

Also $d = 1\,in \times \dfrac{1\,ft}{12\,in} \times \dfrac{1\,m}{3.28\,ft} = 0.0254\,m$

Therefore $Q = A\,v = \dfrac{\pi}{4}d^2\,v = \dfrac{\pi}{4} \times 0.0254^2 \times 12.2 = \underline{0.00618\,^{m^3}/_s}$

3-49. Writing Bernoulli's Equation between stations 1 and 2, we have:

$$Z_1 + \frac{P_1}{\gamma} + \frac{v_1^2}{2g} + H_p - H_m - H_L = Z_2 + \frac{P_2}{\gamma} + \frac{v_2^2}{2g}$$

We have $H_m = 0$, $v_1 = 0$, $Z_2 - Z_1 = 20$, $H_L = 40\,ft$ and $P_1 = 0$.

Substituting known values we have:

$$Z_1 + 0 + 0 + H_p - 0 - 40 = Z_2 + \frac{P_2}{\gamma} + \frac{v_2^2}{2g}$$

Knowing that $Z_2 - Z_1 = 20\,ft$, we have:

$$\frac{P_2}{\gamma} = H_p - \frac{v_2^2}{2g} - 60 \qquad \text{Then using Equation 3-25 yields:}$$

$$H_p = \frac{3950 \times 4}{25 \times 0.9} = 702.2\,ft \quad \text{Next solve for } v_2 \text{ u sin g Eqn. } 3-26.$$

$$v_2 = \frac{0.408\,Q}{D^2} = \frac{0.408 \times 25}{0.75^2} = 18.1 \,^{ft}/_s$$

Substituting values we have:

$$\frac{P_2}{\gamma} = 702.2 - \frac{18.1^2}{2 \times 32.2} - 60 = 702.2 - 5.09 - 60 = 637.1\,ft$$

$$P_2 = 637.1\,ft \times \gamma \left(\frac{lb}{ft^3}\right) = 637.1 \times 0.9 \times 62.4 = 35{,}780 \,\frac{lb}{ft^2}$$

Changing to units of psi yields: $P_2 = \dfrac{35{,}780}{144} = \underline{248 \text{ psi}}$

3-50.   (a) Writing Bernoulli's Equation between stations 1 and 2 we have:

$$Z_1 + \frac{P_1}{\gamma} + \frac{v_1^2}{2g} + H_P - H_m - H_L = Z_2 + \frac{P_2}{\gamma} + \frac{v_2^2}{2g}$$

We have $H_m = 0$, $v_1 = 0$, $Z_1 - Z_2 = 10 \text{ ft}$, $H_L = 0$ and $P_1 = 10 \times 144$

$$= 1440 \frac{\text{lb}}{\text{ft}^2}$$

Since there is no pump between stations 1 and 2, $H_P = 0$.

Solving for v_2 we have:

$$v_2 = \frac{0.408\,Q}{D^2} = \frac{0.408 \times 30}{1.5^2} = 5.44 \frac{\text{ft}}{\text{s}}$$

Substituting known values, we have:

$$Z_1 + \frac{1440}{62.4 \times 0.9} + 0 + 0 - 0 - 0 = Z_2 + \frac{P_2}{\gamma} + \frac{5.44^2}{64.4}$$

Knowing that $Z_1 - Z_2 = 10 \text{ ft}$, we have:

$$\frac{P_2}{\gamma} = 10 + \frac{1440}{62.4 \times 0.9} - \frac{5.44^2}{64.4} = 10 + 25.6 - 0.5 = 35.1 \text{ ft}$$

Thus $P_2 = 35.1 \text{ ft} \times \dfrac{0.9 \times 62.4 \dfrac{\text{lb}}{\text{ft}^3}}{\dfrac{144 \text{ in}^2}{1 \text{ ft}^2}} = \underline{13.7 \text{ psig}}$

(b) In this case, $H_L = 25 \text{ ft}$. Therefore we have from the previous equation:

$$\frac{P_2}{\gamma} = 10 + 25.6 - 0.5 - 25 = 10.1 \text{ ft}$$

$$P_2 = 10.1 \times 0.9 \times \frac{62.4}{144} = \underline{3.94 \text{ psig}}$$

3-51. Writing Bernoulli's Equation between stations 1 and 2 we have:

$$Z_1 + \frac{P_1}{\gamma} + \frac{v_1^2}{2g} + H_P - H_m - H_L = Z_2 + \frac{P_2}{\gamma} + \frac{v_2^2}{2g}$$

We have $H_m = 0$, $v_1 = 0$, $Z_2 - Z_1 = 6.096$ m, $H_L = 12.19$ m and $P_1 = 0$.

Substituting known values we have:

$$Z_1 + 0 + 0 + H_P - 0 - 12.19 = Z_2 + \frac{P_2}{\gamma} + \frac{v_2^2}{2g}$$

Knowing that $Z_2 - Z_1 = 6.096$ m, we have:

$$\frac{P_2}{\gamma} = H_P - \frac{v_2^2}{2g} - 18.29 \qquad \text{We next solve for the pump head.}$$

$$H_P(m) = \frac{\text{Pump Power (W)}}{\gamma\left(\frac{N}{m^3}\right) \times Q\left(\frac{m^3}{s}\right)} = \frac{2984}{(0.9 \times 9797) \times 0.00158} = 214.3 \text{ m}$$

Next solve for v_2 and $\frac{v_2^2}{2g}$:

$$v_2\left(\frac{m}{s}\right) = \frac{Q\left(\frac{m^3}{s}\right)}{A\left(m^2\right)} = \frac{0.00158}{\frac{\pi}{4}\left(0.01905 \text{ m}\right)^2} = 5.54 \frac{m}{s}$$

$$\frac{v_2^2}{2g} = \frac{\left(5.54 \frac{m}{s}\right)^2}{2 \times 9.81 \frac{m}{s^2}} = 1.566 \text{ m} \qquad \text{Substituting values we have.}$$

$$\frac{P_2}{\gamma} = 214.3 - 1.566 - 18.29 = 194.4 \text{ m}$$

$$P_2\left(\frac{N}{m^2}\right) = 194.4 \text{ m} \times \gamma\left(\frac{N}{m^3}\right) = 194.4 \text{ m} \times 8817 \frac{N}{m^3} = 1{,}714{,}000 \frac{N}{m^2}$$

$$= \underline{1714 \text{ kPa}}$$

3-52. (a) Writing Bernoulli's Equation between stations 1 and 2 we have:

37

$$Z_1 + \frac{P_1}{\gamma} + \frac{v_1^2}{2g} + H_P - H_m - H_L = Z_2 + \frac{P_2}{\gamma} + \frac{v_2^2}{2g}$$

We have $H_m = 0$, $v_1 = 0$, $Z_1 - Z_2 = 3.0489$ m, $H_L = 0$ and
$$P_1 = 68.97 \text{ kPa}$$

Since there is no pump between stations 1 and 2, $H_P = 0$.

Solving for v_2 we have:

$$v_2 \left(\frac{m}{s}\right) = \frac{Q\left(\frac{m^3}{s}\right)}{A(m^2)} = \frac{0.001896 \frac{m^3}{s}}{\frac{\pi}{4}(0.0381 \text{ m})^2} = 1.66 \frac{m}{s}$$

Substituting known values we have:

$$Z_1 + \frac{68,970 \frac{N}{m^2}}{8,817 \frac{N}{m^3}} + 0 + 0 - 0 - 0 = Z_2 + \frac{P_2}{\gamma} + \frac{\left(1.66 \frac{m}{s}\right)^2}{2 \times 9.81 \frac{m}{s^2}}$$

Knowing that $Z_1 - Z_2 = 3.048$ m, we have:

$$\frac{P_2}{\gamma} = 3.048 + \frac{68,970}{8,817} - \frac{1.66^2}{2 \times 9.81} = 3.048 + 7.82 - 0.141 = 10.73 \text{ m}$$

$$P_2 = 10.73 \text{ m} \times 8817 \frac{N}{m^3} = 94,610 \frac{N}{m^2} = 94,610 \text{ Pa} = 94.6 \text{ kPa}$$

(b) In this case, $H_L = 7.622$ m. Therefore, we have from the previous equation:

$$\frac{P_2}{\gamma} = 10.73 - 7.622 = 3.11 \text{ m}$$

$$P_2 = 3.11 \times 8817 = 27,400 \text{ Pa} = \underline{27.4 \text{ kPa}}$$

3-53. Per continuity equation: $Q_{in} = Q_{out} = \underline{30 \text{ gpm}}$

(a) Per Bernoulli's equation: $\underline{P_B - P_A = 0}$

(b) Writing Bernoulli's equation we have:

$$Z_A + \frac{P_A}{\gamma} + \frac{v_A^2}{2g} + H_P = Z_B + \frac{P_B}{\gamma} + \frac{v_B^2}{2g}$$

where $\quad H_P = \dfrac{3950 \times HP}{Q\, S_g} = \dfrac{3940 \times 2}{30 \times 0.9} = 293\,ft$

$$v = \frac{0.408\, Q}{D^2} \qquad so \quad v_A = \frac{0.408 \times 30}{2^2} = 3.06\ ^{ft}/_s$$

$$and \quad v_B = \frac{0.408 \times 30}{1^2} = 12.2\ ^{ft}/_s$$

Substituting values we have:

$$\frac{P_B - P_A}{\gamma} = H_P + \frac{v_A^2 - v_B^2}{2g} = 293 + \frac{3.06^2 - 12.2^2}{2 \times 32.2} = 291\,ft$$

$$P_B - P_A = 291\,\gamma = 291 \times 56.2 = 16{,}350\ ^{lb}/_{ft^2} = \underline{114\ psi}$$

3-54. $\quad Q_{in} = Q_{out} = 0.0000632\, Q\,(gpm) = 0.0000632 \times 30 = \underline{0.00190\ ^{m^3}/_s}$

$$d_A = 2\,in = 0.0508\,m \quad and \quad d_B = 1\,in = 0.0254\,m$$

(a) Per Bernoulli's equation: $\quad \underline{P_B - P_A = 0}$

(b) Writing Bernoulli's equation we have:

$$Z_A + \frac{P_A}{\gamma} + \frac{v_A^2}{2g} + H_P = Z_B + \frac{P_B}{\gamma} + \frac{v_B^2}{2g}$$

$$Power = 2\,HP \times \frac{747\,W}{1\,HP} = 1494\,W$$

$$H_P(m) = \frac{Pump\ Power(W)}{\gamma\left(\dfrac{N}{m^3}\right) \times Q\left(\dfrac{m^3}{s}\right)} = \frac{1494}{0.9 \times 9800 \times 0.00190} = 89.2\,m$$

$$v_A = \frac{Q}{A} = \frac{0.00190}{\dfrac{\pi}{4}(0.0508)^2} = 0.937\ ^m/_s$$

and $\quad v_B = \dfrac{0.00190}{\dfrac{\pi}{4}(0.0254)^2} = 3.75\,\text{m/s}$

Substituting values we have:

$$\frac{P_B - P_A}{\gamma} = H_P - \frac{v_B^2 - v_A^2}{2g} = 89.2 - \frac{3.75^2 - 0.937^2}{2 \times 9.81} = 88.5\ \text{m}$$

$$P_B - P_A = 88.5\,\gamma = 88.5 \times 9800 \times 0.90 = 781{,}000\ \text{Pa} = \underline{781\,\text{kPa}}$$

CHAPTER 4   THE DISTRIBUTION SYSTEM

4-1.   To carry the fluid from the reservoir through operating
        components and back to the reservoir.

4-2.   <u>20 ft/s</u>

4-3.   <u>4 ft/s</u>

4-4.   Copper promotes the oxidation of petroleum oils.

4-5.   Zinc, magnesium and cadmium.

4-6.   It raises the pressure levels up to 4 times the steady
        state system design values.

4-7.   1. Tensile strength of conductor material.
        2. Conductor outside diameter.
        3. Operating pressure levels.

4-8.   To handle pressure shocks and provide a factor of safety.

4-9.   1. When a joint is taken apart, the pipe must be tightened
           farther to reseal.
        2. Pipes cannot be bent around obstacles.

4-10.   1. Steel pipe.
        2. Steel tubing.
        3. Plastic tubing.
        4. Flexible hose.

4-11.   Average fluid velocity is defined as the volumetric flow
        rate divided by the pipe cross-sectional area.

4-12.   Malleable iron can be used for hydraulic fittings for low-
        pressure lines such as inlet, return and drain lines.

4-13.   Tubing can be bent into almost any shape, thereby reducing
        the number of required fittings. Tubing is also easier to
        handle and can be reused without any sealing problems.

4-14.   Plastic tubing is relatively inexpensive. Also since it
        can readily be bent to fit around obstacles, it is easy to
        handle and can be stored on reels.

4-15. The quick-disconnect coupling is used mainly where a conductor must be frequently disconnected from a component.

4-16. When a joint is taken apart, the pipe must be tightened farther to reseal. This frequently requires replacing some of the pipe with slightly longer sections although this problem has been somewhat overcome by using Teflon tape to reseal the pipe joints.

4-17. Figure 4-10 shows the flared-type fitting which was developed before the compression-type for sealing against high pressures. Figure 4-9 shows a compression-type fitting which can be repeatedly taken apart and reassembled and remain perfectly sealed against leakage.

4-18. Flexible hoses are used when hydraulic components such as actuators are subject to movement.

4-19. 1. Install so there is no kinking during operation of system.
       2. There should always be some slack to relieve any strain and allow for the absorption of pressure surges.
       3. If the hose is subject to rubbing, it should be encased in a protective sleeve.

4-20. Flexible hose is fabricated in layers of elastomer (synthetic rubber) and braided fabric or braided wire which permits operation at higher pressures. The outer layer is normally synthetic rubber and serves to protect the braided layer.

4-21. <u>Increases.</u>

4-22. By nominal size and schedule number.

4-23. Schedule number is a measure of how thick the wall of a pipe is. For a given nominal pipe size, the pipe outside diameter is fixed and changes in schedule number represent different wall thicknesses and thus different pipe inside diameter values. The larger the schedule number, the larger the wall thickness.

4-24. $D = \sqrt{\dfrac{0.408\,Q}{v}} = \sqrt{\dfrac{0.408 \times 20}{4}} = \underline{1.428 \text{ inch inside diameter}}$

4-25. $D = \sqrt{\dfrac{0.408 \times 20}{20}} = 0.639$ inch inside diameter

4-26. Fluid velocity limitation $= 5\,\dfrac{ft}{s} \times \dfrac{1\,m}{3.28\,ft} = 1.52\,\dfrac{m}{s}$

$$ID_{min} = \sqrt{\dfrac{4\,Q}{\pi\,v}} = \sqrt{\dfrac{4 \times 0.002}{\pi \times 1.52}} = 0.0409\,m = 40.9\,mm$$

Select 42 mm ID

4-27. Fluid velocity limitation $= 20\,\dfrac{ft}{s} \times \dfrac{1\,m}{3.28\,ft} = 6.1\,\dfrac{m}{s}$

$$ID_{min} = \sqrt{\dfrac{4\,Q}{\pi\,v}} = \sqrt{\dfrac{4 \times 0.002}{\pi \times 6.1}} = 0.0204\,m = 20.4\,mm$$

Select 22 mm ID

4-28. $v = \dfrac{Q}{A} = \dfrac{Q}{\dfrac{\pi}{4}D^2}$ Answer is: square

4-29. $v = \dfrac{Q}{A} = \dfrac{Q}{\dfrac{\pi}{4}D^2}$ Thus $\dfrac{v_1}{v_2} = \dfrac{D_2^2}{D_1^2} = \left(\dfrac{D_2}{D_1}\right)^2$

$$v_2 = v_1\left(\dfrac{D_1}{D_2}\right)^2 = v_1\left(\dfrac{1}{2}\right)^2 = \dfrac{v_1}{4}$$ Thus answer is: four

4-30. $A = \dfrac{Q}{v}$ or $A(in^2) = \dfrac{Q\left(\dfrac{in^3}{s}\right)}{v\left(\dfrac{in}{s}\right)}$

$$Q\left(\dfrac{in^3}{s}\right) = Q\left(\dfrac{gal}{min}\right) \times \dfrac{231\,in^3}{1\,gal} \times \dfrac{1\,min}{60\,s} = 3.85\,Q(gpm)$$

$$v\left(\dfrac{in}{s}\right) = v\left(\dfrac{ft}{s}\right) \times \dfrac{12\,in}{1\,ft} = 12\,v\left(\dfrac{ft}{s}\right)$$ Thus we have:

$$A(in^2) = \frac{3.85\,Q(gpm)}{12\,v\left(\dfrac{ft}{s}\right)} \qquad so \qquad C_1 = \frac{3.85}{12} = \underline{0.321}$$

Since units are satisfied by the following equation:

$$A(m^2) = \frac{C_2\,Q\left(\dfrac{m^3}{s}\right)}{v\left(\dfrac{m}{s}\right)} \qquad Then\ \underline{C_2 = 1}$$

4-31. First trial: select 1-1/4 in. OD, 1.060 in. ID tube

$$v = \frac{0.408\,Q}{D^2} = \frac{0.408 \times 30}{1.060^2} = 10.9\ {ft}/{s}$$

Second trial: select 1-1/2 in. OD, 1.310 in. ID tube

$$v = \frac{0.408 \times 30}{1.310^2} = 7.13\ {ft}/{s}$$

Third trial: select 5/8 in. OD, 0.435 in. ID tube

$$v = \frac{0.408 \times 30}{0.435^2} = 62.7\ {ft}/{s}$$

Conclusion:

The 1-1/2 in. OD, 1.310 in. ID size produces a velocity of
7.13 ft/s. Therefore need a larger size than given in
Figure 4-7 for the pump inlet. The 1-1/4 in. OD, 1.060 in.
ID size produces a velocity of 10.9 ft/s. Therefore this
size is adequate for the pump outlet. The 5/8 in. OD,
0.435 in. ID size produces a velocity of 62.7 ft/s.
Therefore this size is too small even for the pump outlet.

4-32.

$$Q = 30\,\frac{gal}{min} \times \frac{231\,in^3}{1\,gal} \times \frac{1\,min}{60\,s} \times \left(\frac{1\,m}{39.4\,in}\right)^3 = 0.00189\ {m^3}/{s}$$

$$v = 5\,\frac{ft}{s} \times \frac{1\,m}{3.28\,ft} = 1.52\,\frac{m}{s} \quad \text{and} \quad v = 20\,\frac{ft}{s} = 6.08\,\frac{m}{s}$$

$$\text{Wall thickness} = 0.095\,in \times \frac{1\,mm}{0.0394\,in} = 2.41\,mm$$

Can select from Figure 4-21, tube sizes having a wall thickness greater than 2.41 mm to withstand pressure.

First trial: select 30 mm OD, 3.0 mm wall, 24 mm ID

$$v = \frac{Q}{A} = \frac{0.00189\,\frac{m^3}{s}}{\frac{\pi}{4}\left(0.024\,m\right)^2} = 4.17\,\frac{m}{s}$$

Second trial: select 35 mm OD, 3.0 mm wall, 29 mm ID

$$v = \frac{Q}{A} = \frac{0.00189\,\frac{m^3}{s}}{\frac{\pi}{4}\left(0.029\,m\right)^2} = 2.86\,\frac{m}{s}$$

Third trial: select 42 mm OD, 3.0 mm wall, 36 mm ID

$$v = \frac{Q}{A} = \frac{0.00189\,\frac{m^3}{s}}{\frac{\pi}{4}\left(0.036\,m\right)^2} = 1.86\,\frac{m}{s}$$

Fourth trial: select 28 mm OD, 2.5 mm wall, 23 mm ID

$$v = \frac{Q}{A} = \frac{0.00189\,\frac{m^3}{s}}{\frac{\pi}{4}\left(0.023\,m\right)^2} = 4.54\,\frac{m}{s}$$

Fifth trial: select 25 mm OD, 3.0 mm wall, 19 mm ID

$$v = \frac{Q}{A} = \frac{0.00189\,\frac{m^3}{s}}{\frac{\pi}{4}\left(0.019\,m\right)^2} = 6.67\,\frac{m}{s}$$

Hence use 28 mm OD, 2.5 mm wall, 23 mm ID size tube for the pump outlet.

Since the 42 mm OD, 3.0 mm wall, 36 mm ID size tube produces a velocity of 1.86 m/s, need a larger size tube than given in Figure 4-21 for the pump inlet.

4-33.   First calculate the wall thickness of the tubing:

$$t = \frac{1.250 - 1.060}{2} = 0.095 \text{ in.}$$

Next find the burst pressure for the tubing.

$$BP = \frac{2\,t\,S}{D_i} = \frac{2 \times 0.095 \times 75{,}000}{1.060} = 13{,}440 \text{ psi}$$

Finally calculate the working pressure:

$$WP = \frac{13{,}440}{8} = 1680 \text{ psi}$$

4-34.   Tensile Stress $= \sigma = \dfrac{P\,D_i}{2\,t} = \dfrac{1000 \text{ psi} \times 1.060 \text{ in}}{2\left(\dfrac{1.250 - 1.060}{2} \text{ in}\right)} = 5580 \text{ psi}$

4-35.   First find the minimum inside diameter based on the fluid velocity limitation of 20 ft/s.

$$D = \sqrt{\frac{0.408\,Q}{v}} = \sqrt{\frac{0.408 \times 20}{20}} = 0.639 \text{ in}$$

From Figure 4-7, the smallest acceptable tube size based on flow rate requirements is:

3/4 in. OD, 0.049 in. wall thickness, 0.652 in. ID

Second find the burst pressures and working pressures for the above tubing for SAE 1010 and AISI 4130 materials.

(a) Material is SAE 1010

$$BP = \frac{2\,t\,S}{D_i} = \frac{2 \times 0.049 \times 55{,}000}{0.652} = 8267 \text{ psi}$$

46

$$WP = \frac{8267}{8} = 1030 \text{ psi}$$

This working pressure is adequate since it is greater than 1000 psi.

Use 3/4 in. OD, 0.049 in. wall thickness, 0.652 in. ID

(b) Material is AISI 4130

$$BP = \frac{2 \times 0.049 \times 75{,}000}{0.652} = 11{,}270 \text{ psi}$$

$$WP = \frac{11{,}270}{8} = 1410 \text{ psi} \quad OK$$

Use 3/4 in. OD, 0.049 in. wall thickness, 0.652 in. ID

4-36.

$$BP = \frac{2\,t\,S}{D_i} = \frac{2 \times 0.003 \text{ m} \times 517\,\frac{MN}{m^2}}{0.024 \text{ m}} = 129.3 \text{ MPa}$$

$$WP = \frac{BP}{FS} = \frac{129.3 \text{ MPa}}{8} = 16.2 \text{ MPa} = \underline{162 \text{ Bars}}$$

4-37. Tensile Stress $= \sigma = \dfrac{P\,D_i}{2\,t} = \dfrac{10 \text{ MPa} \times 0.024 \text{ m}}{2 \times 0.003 \text{ m}} = \underline{40 \text{ MPa}}$

4-38. (a) $ID = \sqrt{\dfrac{4 \times 0.001}{\pi \times 6.1}} = 0.0144 \text{ m} = 14.4 \text{ mm}$

From Fig. 4-21 try 15 mm OD, 1.5 mm wall thickness, 12 mm ID tube size.

$$BP = \frac{2 \times 0.0015 \times 379}{0.012} = 94.8 \text{ MPa}$$

$$WP = \frac{94.8}{8} = 11.9 \text{ MPa} = 119 \text{ Bars}$$

OK since the WP is greater than 70 bars.

<u>Thus use 15 mm OD, 1.5 mm wall thickness, 12 mm ID tube.</u>

(b) Try 15 mm OD, 1.5 mm wall thickness, 12 mm ID tube.

$$BP = \frac{2 \times 0.0015 \times 517}{0.012} = 129.3 \text{ MPa}$$

$$WP = \frac{129.3}{8} = 16.2 \text{ MPa} = 162 \text{ Bars}$$

OK since the WP is greater than 70 bars.

<u>Thus use 15 mm OD, 1.5 mm wall thickness, 12 mm ID tube.</u>

4-39. $BP = \dfrac{2\,t\,S}{D_i} = 2\left(\dfrac{D_o - D_i}{2}\right) \times \dfrac{S}{D_i} = \dfrac{\left(D_o - D_i\right)S}{D_i}$

Substituting values we have:

$$8000 = \frac{\left(D_o - 1\right)}{1} \times 55{,}000 = 55{,}000\,D_o - 55{,}000$$

$$D_o = \frac{55{,}000 + 8{,}000}{55{,}000} = \underline{1.145 \text{ in.}}$$

4-40.   From Exercise 4 – 39, $BP = \dfrac{\left(D_o - D_i\right)S}{D_i}$

Substituting values we have:

$$50 = \frac{\left(D_o - 25\right) \times 379}{25} \qquad \text{Thus} \quad D_o = \underline{28.3 \text{ mm}}$$

CHAPTER 5   BASICS OF HYDRAULIC FLOW IN PIPES

5-1.   It is very important to keep all energy losses in a fluid power system to a minimum acceptable level.

5-2.   Laminar flow is characterized by the fluid flowing in smooth layers. In turbulent flow, the movements of a particle becomes random and fluctuate up and down in a direction perpendicular as well as parallel to the mean flow direction. This causes a mixing motion as particles collide.

5-3.   1. If N_R is less than 2000, the flow is laminar.
        2. If N_R is greater than 4000, the flow is turbulent.
        3. Reynolds numbers between 2000 and 4000 cover a transition region between laminar and turbulent flow.

5-4.   Relative roughness is defined as the pipe inside surface roughness divided by the pipe inside diameter.

5-5.   The K factor equals the head loss divided by the velocity head.

5-6.   The equivalent length of a valve or fitting is that length of pipe which, for the same flow rate, produces the same head loss as the valve or fitting.

5-7.   1. Rotameter.
        2. Orifice flow meter.

5-8.   1. Bourdon gage.
        2. Schrader gage.

5-9.   Flow rate measurements are used to evaluate the performance of hydraulic components as well as trouble-shooting a hydraulic system. They can be used to check the volumetric efficiency of pumps and also to determine leakage paths within a hydraulic circuit. Pressure measurements are used for testing and trouble-shooting purposes. They are used to adjust pressure settings of pressure control valves and to determine forces exerted by hydraulic cylinders and torques delivered by hydraulic motors.

5-10. $\Delta P \propto K$,   <u>true</u>

5-11. Easier to read since values are given in digits rather than by a needle pointing along a scale.

5-12. There is a loss in pressure in the direction of flow and the greater the flow rate, the greater the pressure loss (pressure drop). Also the pressure drop is proportional to the square of the flow rate.

5-13. High velocity and large pipe roughness.

5-14. $N_R = \dfrac{7740 \times v\left(\frac{ft}{s}\right) \times D(in)}{v(cS)} = \dfrac{7740 \times 20 \times 1.5}{75} = \underline{3096}$

5-15. $N_R = \dfrac{v\,D}{v} = \dfrac{6\,\frac{m}{s} \times 0.030\,m}{0.0001\,\frac{m^2}{s}} = \underline{1800}$

Since N_R is less than 2000, the flow is laminar.

5-16. $N_R = \dfrac{v\,D}{v}$, increase

5-17. Assuming laminar flow we have:

$$H_L = \dfrac{64}{N_R} \times \dfrac{L}{D} \times \dfrac{v^2}{2g} = \dfrac{64}{3096} \times \dfrac{100}{1.5/12} \times \dfrac{20^2}{64.4} = 102.7\,ft$$

$\Delta P = 0.433 \times H_L \times S_g = 0.433 \times 102.7 \times 0.90 = \underline{40.0\,psi}$

If turbulent flow with smooth pipe we have:

$f = 0.044, \ \Delta P = \underline{85.0\,psi}$

5-18. (a) $N_R = \dfrac{7740 \times 15 \times 0.75}{100} = 871$ la min ar flow

Thus $f = \dfrac{64}{N_R} = \dfrac{64}{871} = \underline{0.0735}$

(b) $N_R = \dfrac{7740 \times 45 \times 0.75}{100} = 2612$

We therefore assume the flow to be turbulent and must calculate the relative roughness of the pipe.

ε (from Figure 5-7) = 0.00015 ft. Thus the relative roughness can now be found.

$$\frac{\varepsilon}{D} = \frac{0.00015}{0.75/12} = 0.0024$$

From the Moody Diagram (Figure 5-8): $f_{turbulent} = \underline{0.046}$

If the flow is laminar, the friction factor is:

$$f_{la\,min\,ar} = \frac{64}{N_R} = \frac{64}{2612} = \underline{0.0245}$$

5-19. $H_L = \dfrac{64}{N_R} \times \dfrac{L}{D} \times \dfrac{v^2}{2g} = \dfrac{64}{1800} \times \dfrac{100\text{ m}}{0.030\text{ m}} \times \dfrac{\left(6\,{}^m\!/_s\right)^2}{2 \times 9.81\,{}^m\!/_{s^2}} = 217.5\text{ m}$

$\Delta P_L = \gamma\,h = (1000\,\dfrac{kg}{m^2} \times 0.90 \times 9.81\,\dfrac{m}{s^2}) \times 217.5\text{ m}$

$\qquad = 1.92\,\dfrac{MN}{m^2} = 1.92\text{ MPa} = \underline{19.2\text{ bars}}$

5-20. (a) $N_R = \dfrac{v\,D}{\nu} = \dfrac{2 \times 0.020}{0.0001} = 400$ la min ar

$\qquad f = \dfrac{64}{N_R} = \dfrac{64}{400} = \underline{0.16}$

(b) $N_R = \dfrac{10 \times 0.020}{0.0001} = 2000$ la min ar

$\qquad f = \dfrac{64}{2000} = \underline{0.032}$

5-21. $\dfrac{\Delta P}{\rho\,g} = H_L = \dfrac{64}{N_R} \times \dfrac{L}{D} \times \dfrac{v^2}{2g} = \dfrac{64}{\dfrac{v\,D\,\rho}{\mu}} \times \dfrac{L}{D} \times \dfrac{v^2}{2g}$

$$\frac{\Delta P}{\rho g} = H_L = \frac{32 \mu L v}{\rho g D^2} \quad \text{so} \quad \Delta P = \frac{32 \mu L v}{D^2}$$

Hence for laminar flow, ΔP is <u>proportional</u> to v.

5-22. $\quad \dfrac{\Delta P}{\rho g} = H_L = f \times \dfrac{L}{D} \times \dfrac{v^2}{2g} \quad \text{so} \quad \Delta P = \dfrac{\rho f L v^2}{2 D}$

Thus ΔP varies as the <u>square</u> of the velocity (provided the flow is fully turbulent where f is a constant).

5-23. $\quad H_L = K \times \dfrac{v^2}{2g} \qquad$ First calculate the velocity.

$$v = \frac{0.408 \times 100}{1.5^2} = 18.1 \text{ ft}/_s$$

From Figure 5-9, K for a wide open gate valve is 0.19.

$$H_L = 0.19 \times \frac{18.1^2}{64.4} = \underline{0.97 \text{ ft of oil}}$$

5-24. $\quad H_L = K \times \dfrac{v^2}{2g} \quad$ and $\quad K = 0.19$

$$v = \frac{Q}{A} = \frac{0.004 \text{ m}^3/_s}{\frac{\pi}{4}\left(0.030 \text{ m}\right)^2} = 5.66 \text{ m}/_s$$

Thus $H_L = 0.19 \times \dfrac{5.66^2}{2 \times 9.81} = 0.31 \text{ m}$ and the pressure loss is:

$$\Delta P_L = \gamma h = (1000 \times 0.90 \times 9.81) \times 0.31 = 2740 \text{ N}/_{m^2} = \underline{0.0274 \text{ bars}}$$

5-25. $\quad \Delta P \propto Q^2, \quad \underline{\text{factor is 4}}$

5-26. $\quad Q = 38.06 \, C \, A \sqrt{\dfrac{\Delta P}{S_g}} \quad$ Substituting values we have:

$$60 = 38.06\, C \times 0.5 \sqrt{\frac{40}{0.90}} \qquad \text{Thus} \quad C = \underline{0.473}$$

$$\frac{\Delta P}{\gamma} = H_L = K \times \frac{v^2}{2g} \qquad \text{so} \quad K = \frac{2g\, \Delta P}{\gamma\, v^2}$$

where $g = 32.2\, \text{ft}/\text{s}^2$, $\Delta P = 40 \times 144 = 5760\, \text{lb}/\text{ft}^2$ and

$$\gamma = 0.9 \times 62.4 = 56.2\, \text{lb}/\text{ft}^3$$

$$v = \frac{Q}{A} = \frac{60\, \dfrac{\text{gal}}{\text{min}} \times \dfrac{231\, \text{in}^3}{1\, \text{gal}} \times \dfrac{1\, \text{ft}^3}{1728\, \text{in}^3} \times \dfrac{1\, \text{min}}{60\, \text{s}}}{0.5\, \text{in}^2 \times \dfrac{1\, \text{ft}^2}{144\, \text{in}^2}} = \frac{0.134\, \text{ft}^3/\text{s}}{0.00347\, \text{ft}^2}$$

$$= 38.6\ \text{ft/s}$$

$$\text{Thus} \quad K = \frac{2 \times 32.2 \times 5760}{56.2 \times 38.6^2} = \underline{4.43}$$

5-27. The flow coefficient and K factor values would be the same because these two parameters are dimensionless.

5-28. First find the velocity.

$$v = \frac{0.408 \times 30}{0.75^2} = 21.8\ \text{ft}/\text{s}$$

Next find the Reynolds Number.

$$N_R = \frac{7740 \times 21.8 \times 0.75}{75} = 1687$$

Then find the friction factor.

$$f = \frac{64}{N_R} = \frac{64}{1687} = 0.0379$$

Finally we calculate the equivalent length where the K factor equals 0.19 from Figure 5-9.

$$L_e = \frac{KD}{f} = \frac{0.19 \times \dfrac{0.75}{12}}{0.0379} = \underline{0.313 \text{ ft}}$$

5-29. $N_R = \dfrac{vD}{\nu}$ where $v = \dfrac{Q}{A} = \dfrac{0.002}{\dfrac{\pi}{4} \times 0.020^2} = 6.37 \text{ } \dfrac{m}{s}$

$$N_R = \frac{6.37 \times 0.020}{0.0001} = 1274 \quad \text{and} \quad f = \frac{64}{1274} = 0.0502$$

Thus $L_e = \dfrac{KD}{f} = \dfrac{0.19 \times 0.020}{0.0502} = \underline{0.076 \text{ m}}$

5-30. For the system of Figure 5-20, we have the following data:

$H_m = 0$ between stations 1 and 2, $v_1 = 0$, $\dfrac{P_1}{\gamma} = 0$ and

$Z_2 - Z_1 = 20$ ft.

Writing Bernoulli's equation between stations 1 and 2, we have:

$$Z_1 + \frac{P_1}{\gamma} + \frac{v_1^2}{2g} + H_P - H_m - H_L = Z_2 + \frac{P_2}{\gamma} + \frac{v_2^2}{2g}$$

Let's first solve for v_2: $v_2 = \dfrac{0.408 \times 25}{0.75^2} = 18.1 \text{ } \dfrac{ft}{s}$

The velocity head at station 2 is: $\dfrac{v_2^2}{2g} = \dfrac{18.1^2}{64.4} = 5.09 \text{ ft}$

Reynolds Number can now be found.

$$N_R = \frac{7740 \times v\left(\dfrac{ft}{s}\right) \times D(in)}{\nu(cS)} = \frac{7740 \times 18.1 \times 0.75}{75} = 1400$$

The flow is laminar. Thus $f = \dfrac{64}{N_R} = \dfrac{64}{1400} = 0.0457$

We can now find the head loss due to friction between stations 1 and 2.

$$H_L = f \times \frac{L}{D} \times \frac{v^2}{2g} \qquad \text{where} \quad L \text{ is found as follows:}$$

$$L = 16 + 1 + 4 + \left(\frac{KD}{f}\right)_{\text{std elbow}} = 21 + \frac{0.9 \times \dfrac{0.75}{12}}{0.0457} = 22.2 \text{ ft}$$

$$H_L = 0.0457 \times \frac{22.2}{0.75 \Big/ 12} \times 5.09 = 82.6 \text{ ft}$$

We can now substitute values into Bernoulli's equation to solve for $P_2 \big/ \gamma$.

$$\frac{P_2}{\gamma} = \left(Z_1 - Z_2\right) + H_P + \frac{P_1}{\gamma} - H_L - \frac{v_2^2}{2g}$$

$$\frac{P_2}{\gamma} = -20 + H_P + 0 - 82.6 - 5.09 = H_P - 107.7$$

Using Equation 3-25 allows us to solve for the pump head.

$$H_P = \frac{3950 \times HP}{Q \, S_g} = \frac{3950 \times 4}{25 \times 0.9} = 702.2 \text{ ft}$$

Thus we can solve for the pressure head at station 2.

$$\frac{P_2}{\gamma} = 702.2 - 107.7 = 594.5 \text{ ft of oil} = H \text{ ft of oil}$$

Finally we solve for the pressure at station 2.

$$P_2 = 0.433 \, H \, S_g = 0.433 \times 594.5 \times 0.9 = \underline{231.7 \text{ psi}}$$

5-31. For the system of Figure 5-31, we have the following data:

$H_m = 0$, $v_1 = 0$, $Z_1 - Z_2 = 10$ ft and $H_P = 0$ between stations 1 and 2.

Writing Bernoulli's equation between stations 1 and 2, we have:

$$Z_1 + \frac{P_1}{\gamma} + \frac{v_1^2}{2g} + H_P - H_m - H_L = Z_2 + \frac{P_2}{\gamma} + \frac{v_2^2}{2g}$$

Let's first solve for v_2: $\quad v_2 = \dfrac{0.408 \times 30}{1.5^2} = 5.44 \dfrac{ft}{s}$

The velocity head at station 2 is: $\quad \dfrac{v_2^2}{2g} = \dfrac{5.44^2}{64.4} = 0.46 \ ft$

The pressure head at station 1 is: $\quad \dfrac{P_1}{\gamma} = \dfrac{10 \times 144}{62.4 \times 0.9} = 25.6 \ ft$

The Reynolds Number can now be found.

$$N_R = \frac{7740 \ v\left(\frac{ft}{s}\right) \times D(in)}{v(cS)} = \frac{7740 \times 5.44 \times 1.5}{100} = 632$$

The flow is laminar so the friction factor is:

$$f = \frac{64}{N_R} = \frac{64}{632} = 0.101$$

We can now find the head loss due to friction between stations 1 and 2.

$$H_L = f \times \frac{L}{D} \times \frac{v^2}{2g} + \text{head loss across the strainer}$$

where $\quad L = 20 + 3 \times \left(\dfrac{K\,D}{f}\right)_{std\ elbow} = 20 + 3 \times \dfrac{0.9 \times \frac{1.5}{12}}{0.101} = 23.3 \ ft$

Head loss across strainer $= \dfrac{\left(\Delta P\right)_{strainer}}{0.433 \ S_g} = \dfrac{1}{0.433 \times 0.9} = 2.6 \ ft$

$$H_L = 0.101 \times \frac{23.3}{\frac{1.5}{12}} \times 0.46 + 2.6 = 8.6 + 2.6 = 11.2 \ ft$$

We can now substitute into Bernoulli' equation to solve for $\frac{P_2}{\gamma}$.

$$\frac{P_2}{\gamma} = \left(Z_1 - Z_2\right) + \frac{P_1}{\gamma} - H_L - \frac{v_2^2}{2g}$$

$$= 10 + 25.6 - 11.2 - 0.46 = 23.9 \text{ ft of oil} = H \text{ ft of oil}$$

Finally we can solve for the pressure at station 2.

$$P_2 = 0.433 \, H \, S_g = 0.433 \times 23.9 \times 0.9 = \underline{9.31 \text{ psi}}$$

5-32. For the system of Figure 5-20, we have the following data:

$H_m = 0$ between stations 1 and 2, $v_1 = 0$, $\frac{P_1}{\gamma} = 0$ and

$Z_2 - Z_1 = 6.096 \text{ m}$

Writing Bernoulli's equation between stations 1 and 2 we have:

$$Z_1 + \frac{P_1}{\gamma} + \frac{v_1^2}{2g} + H_P - H_m - H_L = Z_2 + \frac{P_2}{\gamma} + \frac{v_2^2}{2g}$$

Let's first solve for v_2: $v_2 = \dfrac{0.00158}{\dfrac{\pi}{4} \times 0.01905^2} = 5.54 \text{ }\frac{m}{s}$

The velocity head at station 2 is: $\dfrac{v_2^2}{2g} = \dfrac{5.54^2}{2 \times 9.81} = 1.57 \text{ m}$

The Reynolds Number can now be found where the kinematic viscosity is:

$$v\left(\frac{m^2}{s}\right) = \frac{v \text{ (cS)}}{1,000,000} = \frac{75}{1,000,000} = 75 \times 10^{-6} \text{ }\frac{m^2}{s}$$

$$N_R = \frac{v\left(\frac{m}{s}\right) \times D(m)}{v\left(\frac{m^2}{s}\right)} = \frac{5.54 \times 0.01905}{75 \times 10^{-6}} = 1400$$

The flow is laminar so the friction depends only on N_R.

Therefore $\quad f = \dfrac{64}{N_R} = \dfrac{64}{1400} = 0.0457$

We can now find the head loss due to friction between stations 1 and 2.

$$H_L = f \times \dfrac{L}{D} \times \dfrac{v^2}{2g} \qquad \text{where}$$

$$L = 4.88 + 0.305 + 1.22 + \left(\dfrac{K\,D}{f}\right)_{\text{std elbow}} = 6.41 + \dfrac{0.9 \times 0.01905}{0.4057}$$

$$= 6.79 \text{ m}$$

$$H_L = 0.0457 \times \dfrac{6.79}{0.01905} \times 1.57 = 25.6 \text{ m}$$

Next use Bernoulli's equation to solve for $\dfrac{P_2}{\gamma}$.

$$\dfrac{P_2}{\gamma} = \left(Z_1 - Z_2\right) + H_P + \dfrac{P_1}{\gamma} - \dfrac{v_2^2}{2g} - H_L = -6.096 + H_P + 0 - 25.6 - 1.57$$

$$= H_P - 33.2$$

Solving for the pump head we have:

$$H_P(m) = \dfrac{\text{Pump Power(Watts)}}{\gamma\left(\dfrac{N}{m^3}\right) \times Q\left(\dfrac{m^3}{s}\right)} = \dfrac{2984}{8817 \times 0.00158} = 214.3 \text{ m}$$

Next we solve for the pressure head at station 2.

$$\dfrac{P_2}{\gamma} = 214.3 - 33.2 = 181.1 \text{ m of oil}$$

Finally we solve for the pressure at station 2.

$$P_2 = 181.1 \text{ m} \times 8817 \; \dfrac{N}{m^3} = 1{,}600{,}000 \text{ Pa} = \underline{1600 \text{ kPa}}$$

5-33. For the system of Figure 5-31 we have the following data:

$H_m = 0$, $v_1 = 0$, $Z_1 - Z_2 = 3.048$ m and $H_P = 0$ between stations 1 and 2.

Writing Bernoulli's equation stations 1 and 2, we have:

$$Z_1 + \frac{P_1}{\gamma} + \frac{v_1^2}{2g} + H_P - H_m - H_L = Z_2 + \frac{P_2}{\gamma} + \frac{v_2^2}{2g}$$

Let's first solve for v_2: $\quad v_2 = \dfrac{0.001896}{\dfrac{\pi}{4} \times 0.0381^2} = 1.66 \ \text{m/s}$

The velocity head at station 2 is: $\quad \dfrac{v_2^2}{2g} = \dfrac{1.66^2}{2 \times 9.81} = 0.141$ m

The pressure head at station 1 is: $\quad \dfrac{P_1}{\gamma} = \dfrac{68,970}{8817} = 7.82$ m

The Reynolds Number can now be found:

$$N_R = \frac{v\left(\text{m/s}\right) \times D(\text{m})}{v\left(\text{m}^2/\text{s}\right)} = \frac{1.66 \times 0.0381}{100/1,000,000} = 632$$

The flow is laminar so $\quad f = \dfrac{64}{N_R} = \dfrac{64}{632} = 0.101$

We can now find the head loss due to friction between stations 1 and 2.

$$H_L = f \times \frac{L}{D} \times \frac{v^2}{2g} + \text{head loss across strainer}$$

where $L = 6.097 + 3\left(\dfrac{K D}{f}\right)_{\text{std elbow}} = 6.097 + 3 \times \dfrac{0.9 \times 0.0381}{0.101}$

$$= 7.12 \ \text{m}$$

Head loss across strainer $= \dfrac{\left(\Delta P\right)_{\text{strainer}}}{\gamma} = \dfrac{6897}{8817} = 0.782$ m

$$H_L = 0.101 \times \frac{7.12}{0.0381} \times 0.141 + 0.782 = 3.44 \text{ m}$$

Next use Bernoulli's equation to solve for $\frac{P_2}{\gamma}$.

$$\frac{P_2}{\gamma} = \left(Z_1 - Z_2\right) + \frac{P_1}{\gamma} - H_L - \frac{v_2^2}{2g} = 3.048 + 7.82 - 3.44 - 0.141$$
$$= 7.29 \text{ m of oil}$$

Finally we can solve for the pressure at station 2.

$$P_2 = 7.29 \times 8817 = 64{,}300 \text{ Pa} = \underline{64.3 \text{ kPa}}$$

5-34.
$$v\left(\frac{ft}{s}\right) = \frac{0.408 \, Q(gpm)}{[D(in)]^2} = \frac{0.408 \times 40}{1^2} = 16.3 \frac{ft}{s}$$

$$N_R = \frac{7740 \, v\left(\frac{ft}{s}\right) \times D(in)}{v(cS)} = \frac{7740 \times 16.3 \times 1}{100} = 1262$$

$$f = \frac{64}{N_R} = \frac{64}{1262} = 0.0507$$

$$L_{eT} = L_{pipe} + \left(\frac{K \, D}{f}\right)_{valve} = 50 + \frac{10 \times \frac{1}{12}}{0.0507} = 50 + 16.4 = 66.4 \text{ ft}$$

$$H_{LT} = f \times \frac{L_{eT}}{D} \times \frac{v^2}{2g} = 0.0507 \times \frac{66.4}{\frac{1}{12}} \times \frac{16.3^2}{64.4} = 167 \text{ ft of oil}$$

$$\left(\Delta P\right)_{psi} = P_1 - P_2 = 0.433 \times 167 \times 0.9 = 65.1 \text{ psi}$$

$$P_2 - P_1 = \underline{-65.1 \text{ psi}}$$

5-35.
$$v = \frac{Q}{A} = \frac{0.0025}{\frac{\pi}{4} \times 0.025^2} = 5.09 \frac{m}{s}$$

$$N_R = \frac{5.09 \times 0.025}{0.0001} = 1272$$

$$f = \frac{64}{1272} = 0.0503$$

$$L_{e\,T} = 16 + \frac{10 \times 0.025}{0.0503} = 16 + 5.0 = 21.0 \text{ m}$$

$$H_{L\,T} = 0.0503 \times \frac{21.0}{0.025} \times \frac{5.09^2}{2 \times 9.81} = 55.8 \text{ m of oil}$$

$$\Delta P = \gamma\, H_{L\,T} = (1000 \times 0.9 \times 9.81) \times 55.8 = 493{,}000 \; \frac{N}{m^2}$$

$$P_2 - P_1 = -\left(\Delta P\right) = -493 \text{ kPa} = \underline{-4.93 \text{ bars}}$$

5-36.
$$v = \frac{0.408 \times 30}{1.5^2} = 5.44 \; \frac{ft}{s}$$

$$N_R = \frac{7740 \times 5.44 \times 1.5}{100} = 632$$

$$f = \frac{64}{632} = 0.101$$

$$L_e = L_{pipe} + \left(\frac{K\,D}{f}\right)_{valve} + 2\left(\frac{K\,D}{f}\right)_{elbow}$$

$$= 45 + \frac{10 \times 1.5}{0.001 \times 12} + 2 \times \frac{0.75 \times 1.5}{0.101 \times 12} = 45 + 12.4 + 1.9 = 59.3 \text{ ft}$$

$$H_L = 0.101 \times \frac{59.3}{1.5/12} \times \frac{5.44^2}{64.4} = 22.0 \text{ ft of oil}$$

$$\Delta P = 0.433 \times 22.0 \times 0.9 = 8.6 \text{ psi} \quad \text{Thus } P_2 = \underline{91.4 \text{ psi}}$$

5-37.
$$v = \frac{Q}{A} = \frac{0.002}{\dfrac{\pi}{4} \times 0.038^2} = 1.76 \; \frac{m}{s}$$

$$N_R = \frac{1.76 \times 0.038}{0.0001} = 669$$

$$f = \frac{64}{669} = 0.096$$

$$L_e = 15 + \frac{10 \times 0.038}{0.096} + 2 \times \frac{0.75 \times 0.038}{0.096} = 15 + 4.0 + 0.6 = 19.6 \text{ m}$$

$$H_L = 0.096 \times \frac{19.6}{0.038} \times \frac{1.76^2}{2 \times 9.81} = 7.82 \text{ ft of oil}$$

$$\Delta P = \gamma H_L = (1000 \times 0.9 \times 9.81) \times 7.82 = 69{,}000 \text{ N}/\text{m}^2 = 0.69 \text{ bars}$$

Therefore $P_2 = \underline{6.31 \text{ bars}}$

5-38. $H_L = \displaystyle\sum_{1}^{13} \left(f \frac{L}{D} \right) \frac{v^2}{2g}$ and $v = \dfrac{0.408\,Q}{D^2}$

$$Q_{\text{return line}} = 40 \left(\frac{8^2 - 4^2}{8^2} \right) = 30 \text{ gpm}$$

$$v_{1,2,3} = \frac{0.408 \times 40}{1.5^2} = 7.25 \text{ ft}/\text{s}$$

$$v_{4,5,6} = \frac{0.408 \times 40}{1.0^2} = 16.3 \text{ ft}/\text{s}$$

$$v_{7,8} = \frac{0.408 \times 30}{1.0^2} = 12.2 \text{ ft}/\text{s}$$

$$v_{9,10} = \frac{0.408 \times 40}{0.75^2} = 29.0 \text{ ft}/\text{s}$$

$$v_{11,12,13} = \frac{0.408 \times 30}{0.75^2} = 21.8 \text{ ft}/\text{s}$$

Now since $N_R = \dfrac{v\,D}{\nu}$, we have:

$$N_{R\,1,2,3} = \frac{7.25 \times 1.5/12}{0.001} = 906 \,, \quad N_{R\,4,5,6} = \frac{16.3 \times 1.0/12}{0.001} = 1358$$

$$N_{R\,7,8} = \frac{12.2 \times \frac{1.0}{12}}{0.001} = 1017 \ , \quad N_{R\,9,10} = \frac{29.0 \times \frac{0.75}{12}}{0.001} = 1813$$

$$N_{R\,11,12,13} = \frac{21.8 \times \frac{0.75}{12}}{0.001} = 1363$$

All flows are laminar. Hence $f = \dfrac{64}{N_R}$

$$H_{L\,1,2,3} = \left(\frac{64}{906} \times \frac{10}{\frac{1.5}{12}} + 1.5 \right) \times \frac{7.25^2}{64.4} = 5.84 \text{ ft of oil}$$

$$= \frac{5.84 \text{ ft} \times 50\,\frac{lb}{ft^3}}{144\,\frac{in^2}{ft^2}} = 2.03 \text{ psi} \quad since\ P = \gamma\,h$$

$$H_{L\,4,5,6} = \left(\frac{64}{1358} \times \frac{65}{\frac{1.0}{12}} + 10.5 \right) \times \frac{16.3^2}{64.4} = 195 \text{ ft} = 67.8 \text{ psi}$$

$$H_{L\,7,8} = \left(\frac{64}{1017} \times \frac{10}{\frac{1.0}{12}} + 0.75 \right) \times \frac{12.2^2}{64.4} = 19.1 \text{ ft} = 6.66 \text{ psi}$$

$$H_{L\,9,10} = \left(\frac{64}{1813} \times \frac{10}{\frac{0.75}{12}} + 0.75 \right) \times \frac{29.0^2}{64.4} = 83.6 \text{ ft} = 29.0 \text{ psi}$$

$$H_{L\,11,12,13} = \left(\frac{64}{1363} \times \frac{90}{\frac{0.75}{12}} + 1.5 \right) \times \frac{21.8^2}{64.4} = 510 \text{ ft} = 177 \text{ psi}$$

$$F = \left[1000 - (2.03 + 67.8 + 29.0) \right] \times \frac{\pi}{4}\,8^2 - (6.66 + 177) \times \frac{\pi}{4}\left(8^2 - 4^2 \right)$$

$$F = 45,300 - 6,900 = \underline{38,400 \text{ lb}}$$

5-39. $$HP_{loss} = \frac{\Delta P(psi) \times Q(gpm)}{1714}$$

Using values from Exercise 5-38, we have:

$$HP_{loss} = \frac{(2.03 + 67.8 + 29.0) \times 40}{1714} + \frac{(6.66 + 177) \times 30}{1714}$$

$$= 2.30 + 3.21 = 5.51 \ HP$$

Since 1 HP = 42.4 BTU/min, we have:

Heat generation rate = 42.4 x 5.51 = 234 BTU/min

$$= \underline{14,000 \ BTU/hr}$$

5-40. $Q = Q_{pump} = 40$ gpm for both the extending and retracting speeds of the cylinder. Thus we have:

$$V_{extending} = \frac{Q}{A_{piston}} = \frac{40 \frac{gal}{min} \times \frac{231 \ in^3}{1 \ gal} \times \frac{1 \ min}{60 \ s}}{\frac{\pi}{4}\left(8 \ in\right)^2} = \frac{154 \frac{in^3}{s}}{50.3 \ in^2}$$

$$= 3.06 \ in/s = \underline{0.255 \ ft/s}$$

$$V_{retracting} = \frac{Q}{A_{piston} - A_{rod}} = \frac{154 \frac{in^3}{s}}{\frac{\pi}{4}\left(8^2 - 4^2\right)in^2} = \frac{154 \frac{in^3}{s}}{37.7 \ in^2}$$

$$= 4.08 \ in/s = \underline{0.340 \ ft/s}$$

5-41. $\Delta P_{pump} = 1000 \ psi \times \frac{1 \ Pa}{0.000145 \ psi} = 6.90 \ MPa$

$$Q_{pump} = 0.0000632 \times 40 = 0.00253 \ ^{m^3}\!/_s$$

$$v = 0.001 \frac{ft^2}{s} \times \left(\frac{1 \ m}{3.28 \ ft}\right)^2 = 0.0000930 \ ^{m^2}\!/_s$$

$$\gamma = 50 \frac{lb}{ft^3} \times \frac{1 \ N}{0.225 \ lb} \times \left(\frac{3.28 \ ft}{1 \ m}\right)^3 = 7840 \frac{N}{m^3}$$

Cylinder piston diameter $= 8 \ in \times \frac{1 \ ft}{12 \ in} \times \frac{1 \ m}{3.28 \ ft} = 0.203 \ m$

Cylinder rod diameter = 0.102 m

All elbows are 90° with a K factor = 0.75

Pipe lengths and inside diameters are as follows:

Pipe No.	Length(m)	Dia.(m)	Pipe No.	Length(m)	Dia.(m)
1	0.610	0.0381	8	1.52	0.0254
2	1.83	0.0381	9	1.52	0.0190
3	0.610	0.0381	10	1.52	0.0190
4	15.2	0.0254	11	18.3	0.0190
5	3.05	0.0254	12	3.05	0.0190
6	1.52	0.0254	13	6.10	0.0190
7	1.52	0.0254			

The following equations are applicable:

$$H_1 = \sum_{1}^{13}\left(f \times \frac{L}{D} + K\right)\frac{v^2}{2g} \;,\; v = \frac{Q}{A} \;,\; N_R = \frac{vD}{\nu}$$

$$Q_{return\,line} = 0.00253 \times \frac{\left(0.203^2 - 0.102^2\right)}{0.203^2} = 0.00189 \;^{m^3}\!/_s$$

$$v_{1,2,3} = \frac{0.00253}{\dfrac{\pi}{4} \times 0.0381^2} = 2.22 \;^m\!/_s$$

$$v_{4,5,6} = \frac{0.00253}{\dfrac{\pi}{4} \times 0.0254^2} = 4.99 \;^m\!/_s$$

$$v_{7,8} = \frac{0.00189}{\dfrac{\pi}{4} \times 0.0254^2} = 3.73 \;^m\!/_s$$

$$v_{9,10} = \frac{0.00253}{\dfrac{\pi}{4} \times 0.0190^2} = 8.92 \;^m\!/_s$$

$$v_{11,12,13} = \frac{0.00189}{\dfrac{\pi}{4} \times 0.0190^2} = 6.67 \;^m\!/_s$$

$$N_{R\,1,2,3} = \frac{2.22 \times 0.0381}{0.000093} = 909, \quad N_{R\,4,5,6} = \frac{4.99 \times 0.0254}{0.000093} = 1362$$

$$N_{R\,7,8} = \frac{3.73 \times 0.0254}{0.000093} = 1018, \quad N_{R\,9,10} = \frac{8.92 \times 0.019}{0.000093} = 1822$$

$$N_{R\,11,12,13} = \frac{6.67 \times 0.019}{0.000093} = 1363$$

All flows are laminar. Hence $f = \dfrac{64}{N_R}$

$$H_{L\,1,2,3} = \left(\frac{64}{909} \times \frac{3.05}{0.0381} + 1.5 \right) \times \frac{2.22^2}{2 \times 9.81} = 1.79\ m = 14{,}000\ Pa$$

$$H_{L\,4,5,6} = \left(\frac{64}{1362} \times \frac{19.8}{0.0254} + 10.5 \right) \times \frac{4.99^2}{2 \times 9.81} = 59.8\ m = 469{,}000\ Pa$$

$$H_{L\,7,8} = \left(\frac{64}{1018} \times \frac{3.05}{0.0254} + 0.75 \right) \times \frac{3.73^2}{2 \times 9.81} = 5.89\ m = 46{,}200\ Pa$$

$$H_{9,10} = \left(\frac{64}{1822} \times \frac{3.05}{0.019} + 0.75 \right) \times \frac{8.92^2}{2 \times 9.81} = 25.9\ m = 203{,}000\ Pa$$

$$H_{L\,11,12,13} = \left(\frac{64}{1363} \times \frac{27.4}{0.019} + 1.5 \right) \times \frac{6.67^2}{2 \times 9.81} = 157\ m = 1{,}230{,}000\ Pa$$

$$F = \left[6{,}900{,}000 - (14{,}000 + 469{,}000 + 203{,}000) \right] \times \frac{\pi}{4} \times 0.203^2$$

$$- \left(46{,}200 + 1{,}230{,}000 \right) \times \frac{\pi}{4} \left(0.203^2 - 0.102^2 \right)$$

$$= 201{,}000 - 30{,}900 = \underline{170{,}000\ N}$$

5-42.   Power Loss (Watts) $= P\,(Pa) \times Q \left(\frac{m^3}{s} \right)$

Using the values from Exercise 5-41, we have:

Power Loss $= (14{,}000 + 469{,}000 + 203{,}000) \times (0.00253)$

$+ (46{,}200 + 1{,}230{,}000) \times (0.00189)$

$= 1740 + 2410 = 4150\ Watts = \underline{4.15\ kW}$

5-43. $Q_{pump}\left(m^3/s\right) = 0.0000632\,Q(gpm) = 0.0000632 \times 40 = 0.00253\ m^3/s$

$$\text{Cylinder piston diameter} = 8\ \text{in} \times \frac{2.54\ cm}{1\ in} = 20.32\ cm$$

$$V_{extending} = \frac{Q}{A_{piston}} = \frac{0.00253\ m^3/s}{\dfrac{\pi}{4} \times \left(0.2032\ m\right)^2} = \underline{0.0780\ m/s}$$

$$\text{Cylinder rod diameter} = 4\ \text{in} \times \frac{2.54\ cm}{1\ in} = 10.16\ cm$$

$$V_{retracting} = \frac{Q}{A_{piston} - A_{rod}} = \frac{0.00253\ m^3/s}{\dfrac{\pi}{4} \times \left(0.2032^2 - 0.1016^2\right)} = \underline{0.104\ m/s}$$

5-44. $Q = 38.06\,C\,A\sqrt{\dfrac{\Delta P}{S_g}} = 38.06 \times 0.80 \times \dfrac{\pi}{4} \times 2^2 \sqrt{\dfrac{50}{0.9}} = \underline{713\ gpm}$

5-45. $Q = 1.41\,C\,A\sqrt{\dfrac{\Delta P}{S_g}} = 1.41 \times 0.80 \times \dfrac{\pi}{4} \times 0.055^2 \sqrt{\dfrac{300}{0.9}} = \underline{0.0489\ m^3/s}$

5-46. $Q = 38.06 \times 0.80 \times \dfrac{\pi}{4} \times 2^2 \sqrt{\dfrac{\Delta P}{0.9}} = 100.8\sqrt{\Delta P}$

Let's develop a table of values of Q versus ΔP and plot the corresponding curve.

Q (gpm)	ΔP	Q (gpm)	ΔP
0	0	781	60
319	10	843	70
451	20	902	80
552	30	956	90
638	40	1008	100
713	50		

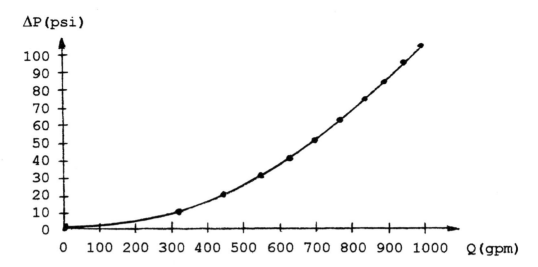

The graph is quicker to use but is not as accurate as the equation. A pressure gage can be calibrated (according to this relationship) to read Q directly rather ΔP.

5-47. In writing the computer program, the following symbols are used:

Elevation(m): Z1, Z2
Pressure(kPa): P1, P2
Velocity(m/s): V1, V2

Acceleration of Gravity $\left(\frac{m}{s^2}\right)$: G

Pump Head(m): PUMPHD
Pump Power(kW): PUMPPRW
Head Loss(m): HL
Reynolds Number: NR
Friction Factor: F
K Factor of Standard Elbow: K
Actual Pipe Length(m): L
Equivalent Pipe Length(m): LEQUIV
Pipe Diameter(m): D

Flow Rate $\left(\frac{m^3}{s}\right)$: Q

Fluid Specific Gravity: SG

Fluid Weight Density $\left(\frac{N}{m^3}\right)$: DENSITY

Fluid Kinematic Viscosity(cS): KINVISC

Fluid Kinematic Viscosity $\left(\frac{m^2}{s}\right)$: KINVISCM

Next we write the problem solving equations using the symbols selected for the computer program.

$$\text{DENSITY} = 9800 \times \text{SG} = 9800 * \text{SG}$$

$$\text{V2} = \frac{4Q}{\pi D^2} = 4 * Q / (3.14 * D^2)$$

$$\text{KINVISCM} = \frac{\text{KINVISC}}{10^6} = 0.000001 * \text{KINVISC}$$

$$\text{NR} = \frac{\text{V2} * \text{D}}{\text{KINVISCM}} = \text{V2} * D / \text{KINVISCM}$$

$$F = \frac{64}{\text{NR}} = 64 / \text{NR}$$

$$\text{LEQUIV} = L + \frac{\text{KD}}{F} = L + K * D / F$$

$$\text{HL} = F\, \frac{L}{D}\left(\frac{\text{V2}^2}{2G}\right) = F * \text{LEQUIV} * \text{V2}^2 / (2 * D * G)$$

$$\text{PUMPHD} = \frac{1000\ \text{PUMPPRW}}{\text{DENSITY} \times Q} = 1000 * \text{PUMPPRW} / (\text{DENSITY} * Q)$$

$$\text{P2} = \text{DENSITY} \times \left(\text{PUMPHD} - \text{HL} - \text{Z2} - \frac{\text{V2}^2}{2G}\right) \times 0.001$$

$$= \text{DENSITY} * \left(\text{PUMPHD} - \text{HL} - \text{Z2} - \text{V2}^2 / (2 * G)\right) * 0.001$$

The computer program is written as follows:

```
PRINT "Computer Anal. of Hydr. System in Fig. 5-20"
PRINT "Press. at Inlet to Hydr. Motor will be Calculated
in Units of kPa"
INPUT "Enter the Pump kW Power:", PUMPPRW
```

INPUT "Enter the Pump Flow Rate $\left(\text{m}^3\middle/\text{s}\right)$:", Q

```
INPUT "Enter the Pipe Diameter(m):", D
INPUT "Enter the K Factor of the STD Elbow:", K
INPUT "Enter the Oil Specific Gravity:", Sg
INPUT "Enter the Kin. Visc. Of Oil(cS):",  KINVISC
INPUT "Enter the Actual Pipe Length(m):", L
INPUT "Enter the Elevation of Hydr. Motor(m):", Z2

G = 9.81
DENSITY = 9800 * SG
V2 = 4 * Q / (3.14 * D^2)
KINVISCM = 0.000001 * KINVISC
NR = V2 * D / KINVISCM
F = 64 / NR
LEQUIV = L + K * D / F
HL = F * LEQUIV * V2^2 / (2 * D * G)
PUMPHD = 1000 * PUMPPRW / (DENSITY * Q)
```

```
P2 = DENSITY * (PUMPHD - HL - Z2 - V2^2 / (2 * G))
```

```
PRINT "The Pressure at the Inlet to the Hydraulic Motor
is"; P2; "kPa"
END
```

(a) The execution of the computer program results in a
    pressure at the inlet to the hydraulic motor of 1795
    kPa. This value agrees with the calculation done
    manually in Example 5-11.

(b) Inputting data values with kinematic viscosity equal
    to 50, 75, 100,125, 150 and 200 cS, yields the
    following results:

Kin. Visc.(cS)	Press. At Hydr. Motor(kPa)
50	1848
75	1821
100	1795
125	1767
150	1741
200	1688

(c) Inputting data values with pump power equal to 3.0,
    3.5, 4.0 and 4.5 kW yields the following results:

Pump Power(kW)	Press. At Hydr. Motor(kPa)
3.0	1410
3.5	1673
4.0	1937
4.5	2201

5-48. Computer Program

5-49. Computer Program

CHAPTER 6   THE SOURCE OF HYDRAULIC POWER: PUMPS

6-1.   1. Gear
       2. Vane
       3. Piston

6-2.   A positive displacement pump ejects a fixed amount of fluid into the hydraulic system per revolution of pump shaft rotation. Thus, for positive displacement pumps, pump flow rate is directly proportional to pump speed. However, for centrifugal pumps, flow output is reduced as circuit resistance is increased. Thus, the flow rate from a centrifugal pump not only depends on the pump speed, but also on the resistance of the external system.

6-3.   All pumps operate on the principle whereby a partial vacuum is created at the pump inlet due to the internal operation of the pump. This allows atmospheric pressure to push the fluid out of the oil tank into the pump intake. The pump then mechanically pushes the fluid out the discharge line as shown by Figure 6-1.

6-4.   Volumetric efficiency equals actual flow rate produced by a pump, divided by the theoretical flow rate based on volumetric displacement and pump speed. Actual flow rate is measured by a flow meter and theoretical flow rate is calculated from the equation: $Q_T = V_D N$

6-5.   Mechanical efficiency is determined by using Equation 6-7 where pump discharge pressure P, pump input torque T and pump speed N are measured. The theoretical pump flow rate is calculated from the equation: $Q_T = V_D N$

6-6.   After the volumetric efficiency η_v and mechanical efficiency η_m have been found, the overall efficiency η_o is determined from the equation: $\eta_o = \eta_v \times \eta_m / 100$

6-7.   A partial vacuum is created at the pump inlet due to the internal operation of the pump (See Figure 6-1). This allows atmospheric pressure to push the fluid out of the oil tank and into the pump intake because atmospheric pressure is greater than vacuum pressure.

6-8.   A fixed displacement pump is one in which the amount of fluid ejected per revolution (displacement) cannot be varied. In a variable displacement pump, the displacement can be varied by changing the physical relationships of various pump elements. This change in pump displacement, produces a change in pump flow output even though pump speed remains constant.

6-9. 1. Spur gear
      2. Helical gear
      3. Herringbone gear

6-10. 1. Lobe
      2. Gerotor

6-11. Three precision ground screws, meshing within a close-fitting housing, deliver non-pulsating flow (See Figure 6-12). The two symmetrically opposed idler rotors are in rolling contact with the central power rotor and are free to float in their respective housing bores on a hydrodynamic oil film.

6-12. 1. Flow rate requirements
      2. Operating speed
      3. Pressure rating
      4. Performance
      5. Reliability
      6. Maintenance
      7. Cost
      8. Noise

6-13. A pressure compensated vane pump is one in which system pressure acts directly on the cam ring via a hydraulic piston (See Figure 6-15). This forces the cam ring against the compensation spring-loaded piston. If the discharge pressure is large enough, it overcomes the compensator spring force and shifts the cam ring. As the discharge pressure continues to increase, zero eccentricity and thus, zero flow is achieved. Therefore, such a pump has its own protection against excessive pressure buildup.

6-14. Pump cavitation occurs when suction lift is excessive and the inlet pressure falls below the vapor pressure of the fluid (usually about 5 psi suction). As a result, vapor bubbles which form in the low pressure inlet region of the pump, are collapsed when they reach the high pressure discharge region. This produces high fluid velocities and impact forces which erode the surfaces of metallic components. The result is shortened pump life.

6-15.   Pumps do not pump pressure. Instead they produce fluid
        flow. The resistance to this flow, produced by the
        hydraulic system, is what determines the pressure.

6-16.   Cavitation can occur due to entrained vapor bubbles. This
        occurs when suction lift is excessive and the inlet
        pressure falls below the vapor pressure of the fluid
        (usually about 5 psi suction). Cavitation produces very
        large fluid impact forces which erodes the surfaces of
        metallic components and thus shortens pump life.

6-17.   If there is no place for the fluid to go, the pressure
        will rise to an unsafe level unless a pressure relief
        valve opens to allow flow back to the oil tank. Thus, the
        relief valve determines the maximum pressure level which
        the system will experience.

6-18.   The flow output of a centrifugal pump is reduced as
        circuit resistance is increased. Therefore, centrifugal
        pumps are rarely used in hydraulic systems.

6-19.   Simplicity in design and compactness in size.

6-20.   A balanced vane pump is one that has two intake and two
        outlet ports diametrically opposite each other. Thus,
        pressure ports are opposite each other and a complete
        hydraulic balance is achieved. This eliminates the bearing
        side loads and, thus, permits higher operating pressures.

6-21.   A pressure intensifier is an auxiliary unit used to
        increase the pressure in a hydraulic system to a value
        above the pump discharge value. It accepts a high volume
        flow at relatively low pump pressure and converts a
        portion of this flow to high pressure. One application is
        for a punch press.

6-22.   1. Axial design
        2. Radial design

6-23.   1. Pump speed
        2. Pressure
        3. Pump size
        4. Entrained gas bubbles

6-24.   The pressure rating is defined as the maximum pressure
        level at which the pump can operate safely and provide a
        good useful life.

6-25.   1. Keep the suction line velocities below 5 ft/s.
         2. Keep the pump inlet lines as short as possible.
         3. Minimize the number of fittings in the inlet line.
         4. Mount the pump as close as possible to the reservoir.

6-26.   Gear pumps are simple in design and compact in size. They
         are the least expensive. Vane pump efficiencies and costs
         fall in between gear and piston pumps. Piston pumps are
         the most expensive and provide the highest level of
         overall performance.

6-27.   Suction pressure because the oil tank is vented to the
         atmosphere and there is a pressure drop in the inlet line
         due to elevation changes, velocity changes and friction.

6-28.   Pumps produce fluid flow. The resistance to this flow,
         produced by the hydraulic system, causes pressure to be
         created. The greater the resistance to flow, the greater
         the pressure.

6-29.   Ejects a fixed amount of fluid per revolution of pump
         shaft rotation. Capable of overcoming the pressure
         resulting from the mechanical loads on the system as well
         as the resistance to flow due to friction

6-30.   By specifying volumetric displacement and volumetric flow
         rate at a given pump speed.

6-31.   Vane and piston pumps.

6-32.   A balanced vane pump is one that has two intake and two
         outlet ports diametrically opposite each other. Thus,
         pressure ports are opposite each other, and a complete
         hydraulic balance is achieved eliminating bearing side
         loads and thus permitting higher operating pressures.

6-33.   By varying the offset angle between the cylinder block
         centerline and the drive shaft centerline.

6-34.   Excessive leakage, distortion of casing and overloading of
         shaft bearings.

6-35.   Change diameter of gear teeth and width of gear teeth.

6-36.   The eccentricity between the centerline of the rotor and
         the centerline of the cam ring can be changed by a hand
         wheel or by a pressure compensator.

6-37.   The addition of pressure compensation prevents the manual
        setting of the rotor eccentricity to vary flow rate.
        Rather, the eccentricity is controlled by pump discharge
        pressure resulting in zero flow rate (zero eccentricity)
        at maximum pump discharge pressure. Thus the pump is
        protected against excessive pressure because it produces
        no flow at the maximum pressure level.

6-38.   Noise is sound that people find undesirable.

6-39.   Intensity and loudness are not the same because loudness
        depends on each person's sense of hearing. The loudness of
        a sound may not be the same for two people sitting next to
        each other and listening to the same sound. However the
        intensity of sound, which represents the amount of energy
        possessed by the sound, can be measured and thus does not
        depend on who hears it.

6-40.   One decibel equals the smallest change in intensity that
        can be detected by most people. The weakest sound
        intensity that the human ear can hear is designated as
        zero decibels. Since one bel represents a very large
        change in sound intensity, it has become standard practice
        to express sound intensity in units of decibels (a bel =
        10 decibels).

6-41.   1. Prolonged exposure to loud noise can result in loss of
           hearing.
        2. Noise can mask sounds that people want to hear. These
           include voice communication between people and warning
           signals emanating from safety equipment.

6-42.   1. Make design changes to the source of the noise such as
           a pump.
        2. Modify the path along which the noise travels such as
           by clamping hydraulic piping at specifically located
           supports.
        3. Use sound absorption materials in nearby screens or
           partitions.

6-43.   Screw pumps increase the fluid pressure less abruptly from
        inlet to outlet than do gear, vane and piston pumps.

6-44. $Q_T = \dfrac{V_D N}{231}$ where $V_D = 9 \times \dfrac{\pi}{4} \times 0.5^2 \times 0.75 = 1.33 \text{ in}^3$

$$Q_T = \frac{1.33 \times 2000}{231} = \underline{11.5 \text{ gpm}}$$

6-45. $\quad e = \dfrac{2 V_D}{\pi \left(D_c + D_R\right) L} = \dfrac{2 \times 7}{\pi (4.5 + 2.5) \times 2} = \underline{0.371 \text{ in}}$

6-46. $\quad \tan \theta = \dfrac{231\,Q}{D\,A\,N\,Y} = \dfrac{231 \times 30}{5 \times \dfrac{\pi}{4}\left(\dfrac{5}{8}\right)^2 \times 3000 \times 9} = 0.167$

Thus $\quad \theta = \underline{9.5°}$

6-47. $\quad Q = S\,A\,N\,Y = 0.020\,\text{m} \times \dfrac{\pi}{4}\left(0.015\,\text{m}\right)^2\left(\dfrac{2000}{60}\,\dfrac{\text{rev}}{\text{s}}\right) \times 9 = 0.00106\,\dfrac{\text{m}^3}{\text{s}}$

6-48. $\quad e = \dfrac{2 V_D}{\pi \left(D_c + D_R\right) L} = \dfrac{2 \times \left(115 \times 10^3\right)}{\pi\,(88.9 + 63.5) \times 50.8} = 9.46 \text{ mm}$

6-49. $\quad \tan \theta = \dfrac{Q}{D\,A\,N\,Y} = \dfrac{0.0019}{0.127 \times \dfrac{\pi}{4}\,(0.0159)^2 \times \dfrac{3000}{60} \times 9} = 0.167$

Thus $\quad \theta = \underline{9.5°}$

6-50. $\quad \eta_v = \dfrac{\text{actual flowrate}}{\text{theoretical flowrate}} \times 100 = \dfrac{Q_A \left(\text{m}^3/\text{min}\right)}{V_D \left(\text{m}^3\right) \times N \left(\text{rev}/\text{min}\right)} \times 100$

Substituting known values, we have:

$$96 = \frac{0.029}{V_D \times 1000} \times 100 \quad \text{Hence} \quad V_D = 0.0000302\,\text{m}^3 = \underline{0.0302 \text{ L}}$$

6-51. $\quad Q\left(\dfrac{\text{m}^3}{\text{min}}\right) = V_D \left(\text{m}^3\right) \times N \left(\dfrac{\text{rev}}{\text{min}}\right)$

6-52. $\quad \eta_o = \dfrac{\eta_V\,\eta_m}{100} \quad$ Thus $\eta_m = 100 \times \dfrac{\eta_o}{\eta_V} = 100 \times \dfrac{88}{92} = \underline{95.7 \text{ \%}}$

6-53. First find the displacement volume.

$$V_D = \frac{\pi}{4} \times \left(3.25^2 - 2.25^2\right) \times 1 = 4.32 \text{ in}^3$$

Next find the theoretical flow rate.

$$Q_T = \frac{V_D \, N}{231} = \frac{4.32 \times 1800}{231} = 33.7 \text{ gpm}$$

The volumetric efficiency can now be found.

$$\eta_v = \frac{29}{33.7} \times 100 = \underline{86.1 \%}$$

6-54.

$$V_D = \frac{\pi}{4}\left(D_o^2 - D_i^2\right) L = \frac{\pi}{4}\left(0.0826^2 - 0.0572^2\right) \times 0.0254 = 70.8 \times 10^{-6} \text{m}^3$$

$$Q_T = V_D \, N = \left(70.8 \times 10^{-6} \text{ m}^3\right) \times \frac{1800}{60} \frac{\text{rev}}{\text{s}} = 2120 \times 10^{-6} \text{ m}^3\!/\!\text{s}$$

$$= 0.00212 \text{ m}^3\!/\!\text{s}$$

$$\eta_v = \frac{0.00183}{0.00212} \times 100 = \underline{86.3 \%}$$

6-55. $\eta_m = \dfrac{\eta_o}{\eta_v} \times 100 = \dfrac{0.88}{0.92} \times 100 = \underline{96 \%}$

Frictional HP = 0.12 x 8 = $\underline{0.96 \text{ HP}}$

6-56. $\eta_o = \dfrac{\text{pump output power}}{\text{pump input power}} \times 100$

$$\text{Output power} = P \, Q = 10 \times 10^6 \, \frac{\text{N}}{\text{m}^2} \times 40 \, \frac{\text{L}}{\text{min}} \times \frac{1 \text{ m}^3\!/\!\text{s}}{1000 \text{ L}\!/\!\text{s}} \times \frac{1 \text{ min}}{60 \text{ s}}$$

$$= 6670 \text{ W} = 6.67 \text{ kW}$$

$$\text{Input power} = 10 \text{ HP} \times \frac{746 \text{ W}}{1 \text{ HP}} = 7460 \text{ W} = 7.46 \text{ kW}$$

$$\eta_o = \frac{6670}{7460} \times 100 = \underline{89.4 \%}$$

6-57. $\text{dB Increase} = 10 \times \log \dfrac{I \text{(final)}}{I \text{(initial)}} = 10 \times \log 10 = \underline{10 \text{ dB}}$

6-58. $\text{HP}_{\text{hydr}} = \dfrac{P\,Q}{1714} = \dfrac{2000 \times 10}{1714} = \underline{11.7 \text{ HP}}$

$\text{HP}_{\text{elec motor}} = \dfrac{\text{HP}_{\text{hydr}}}{\eta_o} = \dfrac{11.7}{0.85} = \underline{13.8 \text{ HP}}$

6-59. (a) First find the theoretical flow rate.

$$Q_T = \frac{V_D\,N}{231} = \frac{6 \times 1000}{231} = 26.0 \text{ gpm}$$

Next solve for the volumetric efficiency.

$$\eta_v = \frac{Q_A}{Q_T} \times 100 = \frac{24}{26.0} \times 100 = 92.3\,\%$$

Then solve for the mechanical efficiency.

$$\eta_m = \frac{P\,Q_T/1714}{T\,N/63{,}000} = \frac{1000 \times 26.0/1714}{1100 \times 1000/63{,}000} \times 100 = \frac{15.17}{17.46} \times 100$$

$$= 86.9\,\%$$

Finally we solve for the overall efficiency.

$$\eta_o = \frac{\eta_v\,\eta_m}{100} = \frac{92.3 \times 86.9}{100} = \underline{80.2\,\%}$$

(b) $T_T = T_A \times \eta_m = 1100 \times 0.869 = \underline{956 \text{ in} \cdot \text{lb}}$

6-60. $\text{Hydraulic Power} = P\,Q = \left(140 \times 10^5\ \dfrac{\text{N}}{\text{m}^2}\right) \times 0.001\ \dfrac{\text{m}^3}{\text{s}}$

$= 14.0 \times 10^3\ \dfrac{\text{N} \cdot \text{m}}{\text{s}} = \underline{14.0 \text{ kW}}$

$\text{Electric Power} = \dfrac{14.0}{0.85} = \underline{16.5 \text{ kW}}$

6-61. (a) $Q_T = V_D N = \left(98.4 \times 10^{-6} \, m^3\right) \times \dfrac{1000}{60} \, \dfrac{rev}{s} = 0.00164 \, m^3\!/s$

$\eta_v = \dfrac{0.00152}{0.00164} \times 100 = 92.7 \, \%$

$\eta_m = \dfrac{P \, Q_T}{T \, \omega} \times 100 = \dfrac{\left(70 \times 10^5 \, N\!/m^2\right) \times 0.00164 \, m^3\!/s}{\left(124.3 \, N \bullet m\right) \times \left(\dfrac{1000}{60} \times 2\pi \, rad\!/s\right)}$

$= 88.2 \, \%$

$\eta_o = \dfrac{\eta_v \, \eta_m}{100} = \dfrac{92.7 \times 88.2}{100} = 81.8 \, \%$

(b) $T_T = T_A \, \eta_m = 124.3 \times 0.882 = \underline{109.6 \, N \bullet m}$

6-62. $\eta_o = \dfrac{\text{pump output HP}}{\text{pump input HP}} \times 100 = \dfrac{P\,Q\!/1714}{10} \times 100$

$= \dfrac{3000 \times 5\!/1714}{10} \times 100 = \underline{87.5 \, \%}$

Pump input HP $= \dfrac{T \, N}{63,000} = \dfrac{T \times 1000}{63,000} = 10$ Thus $T = \underline{630 \, in \bullet lb}$

6-63. $Q_T = \dfrac{V_D \, N}{231} = \dfrac{6 \times 1200}{231} = 31.2 \, gpm$

$\eta_v = \dfrac{Q_A}{Q_T} \times 100 = \dfrac{29}{31.2} \times 100 = 92.9 \, \%$

$\eta_m = \dfrac{\eta_o}{\eta_v} \times 100 = \dfrac{88}{92.9} \times 100 = 94.7 \, \%$

$T_T = \dfrac{V_D \, P}{2\pi} = \dfrac{6 \times 500}{2\pi} = 477.5 \, in \bullet lb$

$T_A = \dfrac{T_T}{\eta_m} = \dfrac{477.5}{0.947} = \underline{504.2 \, in \bullet lb}$

6-64. Prime mover HP $= \dfrac{P\,Q}{1714} = \dfrac{2000 \times 10}{1714} = \underline{11.7\ \text{HP}}$

Prime mover speed $= \dfrac{231\,Q}{V_D} = \dfrac{231 \times 10}{1.5} = \underline{1540\ \text{rpm}}$

6-65. $\dfrac{\text{High Discharge Pressure}}{1000\ \text{psi}} = \dfrac{3}{1} = \dfrac{21}{\text{Low Discharge Flowrate}}$

Solving for the unknown quantities, we have:

High Discharge Pressure $= 3 \times 1000 = \underline{3000\ \text{psi}}$

Low Discharge Flowrate $= 21/3 = \underline{7\ \text{gpm}}$

6-66. $\dfrac{\text{High Discharge Pressure}}{70\ \text{bars}} = \dfrac{3}{1} = \dfrac{0.001\ \text{m}^3/\text{s}}{\text{Low Discharge Flowrate}}$

Low Discharge Flowrate $= \dfrac{0.001}{3} = \underline{0.000333\ \text{m}^3/\text{s}}$

High Discharge Pressure $= 3 \times 70 = \underline{210\ \text{bars}}$

6-67. (a) $Q_{\text{pump act}} = A_{\text{piston}}\,V_{\text{piston ext}}$

$$= \dfrac{\pi}{4} \times 8^2\ \text{in}^2 \times 3\,\dfrac{\text{in}}{\text{s}} \times \dfrac{1\ \text{gal}}{231\ \text{in}^3} \times \dfrac{60\ \text{s}}{1\ \text{min}} = \underline{39.2\ \text{gpm}}$$

$$Q_{\text{pump theor}} = \dfrac{Q_{\text{pump act}}}{\eta_v} = \dfrac{39.2}{0.92} = \underline{42.6\ \text{gpm}}$$

$$Q_{\text{pump theor}} = \dfrac{V_D N}{231} = \dfrac{V_D \times 1800}{231} = 42.6 \quad \text{Thus} \quad V_D = \underline{5.47\ \text{in}^3}$$

(b) $HP_{\text{pump output}} = \dfrac{\left(\Delta P\right) Q_{\text{act}}}{1714}$

$$P_{\text{blank end}}A_{\text{piston}} - P_{\text{rod end}}\left(A_{\text{piston}} - A_{\text{rod}}\right) = F_{\text{ext. load}}$$

$$P_{\text{blank end}} \times \dfrac{\pi}{4}\left(8^2\right) - 50 \times \dfrac{\pi}{4}\left(8^2 - 4^2\right) = 40{,}000$$

Therefore $P_{\text{blank end}}$ = 833 psi

$$HP_{\text{pump output}} = \frac{(833 + 75 + 4) \times 39.2}{1714} = 20.9 \text{ HP}$$

$$HP_{\text{pump input}} = \frac{HP_{\text{pump output}}}{\eta_v \; \eta_m} = \frac{20.9}{0.92 \times 0.90} = \underline{25.2 \text{ HP}}$$

(c) $\quad HP_{\text{pump input}} = \dfrac{T \, N}{63,000}$

$$25.2 = \frac{T \times 1800}{63,000} \qquad \text{Thus} \quad T = \underline{882 \text{ in} \bullet \text{lb}}$$

(d) Power to load = $F_{\text{load}} \; V_{\text{cyl. ext.}}$

$$= 40,000 \text{ lb} \times 3 \frac{\text{in}}{\text{s}} \times \frac{1 \text{ ft}}{12 \text{ in}} \times \frac{1 \text{ HP}}{550 \dfrac{\text{ft} \bullet \text{lb}}{\text{s}}}$$

$$= 18.2 \text{ HP}$$

Percent of pump input power delivered to load

$$= \frac{18.2}{25.2} \times 100 = \underline{72.2 \, \%}$$

6-68. The following metric data are applicable:

Cylinder piston diameter = $8 \text{ in} \times \dfrac{1 \text{ ft}}{12 \text{ in}} \times \dfrac{1 \text{ m}}{3.28 \text{ ft}} = 0.203 \text{ m}$

Cylinder piston rod diameter = 4 in = 0.102 m

Extending speed of cyl. = $3 \dfrac{\text{in}}{\text{s}} \times \dfrac{1 \text{ ft}}{12 \text{ in}} \times \dfrac{1 \text{ m}}{3.28 \text{ ft}} = 0.0762 \dfrac{\text{m}}{\text{s}}$

External load on cyl. = $40,000 \text{ lb} \times \dfrac{1 \text{ N}}{0.225 \text{ lb}} = 178,000 \text{ N}$

Pump volumetric efficiency = 92%

Pump mechanical efficiency = 90%

Pump speed = 1800 rpm

Pump inlet pressure = $-4.0 \text{ psi} \times \dfrac{1 \text{ Pa}}{0.000145 \text{ psi}} = -27{,}600 \text{ Pa}$

Total pressure drop in the line from the pump discharge port to the blank end of the cylinder is:

$75 \text{ psi} \times \dfrac{1 \text{ Pa}}{0.000145 \text{ psi}} = 517{,}000 \text{ Pa}$

Total pressure drop in the return line from the rod end of the cylinder = $50 \text{ psi} \times \dfrac{1 \text{ Pa}}{0.000145 \text{ psi}} = 345{,}000 \text{ Pa}$

(a) $Q_{pump \ act} = A_{piston} \ v_{piston \ ext} = \dfrac{\pi}{4} \times 0.203^2 \times 0.0762 = 0.00247 \ {}^{m^3}\!/_{s}$

$Q_{pump \ theor} = \dfrac{Q_{pump \ act}}{\eta_V} = \dfrac{0.00247}{0.92} = 0.00268 \ {}^{m^3}\!/_{s}$

$Q_{pump \ theor} = V_D \ N = 0.00268$

where $N = 1800 \dfrac{rev}{min} \times \dfrac{1 \ min}{60 \ s} = 30 \ {}^{rev}\!/_{s} = 30 \ {}^{r}\!/_{s}$

Thus $V_D = \dfrac{0.00268}{30} = 0.0000893 \ m^3 = \underline{0.0893 \ L}$

(b) Pump Output Power $= \left(\Delta P \right) Q_{act}$

$P_{blank \ end} A_{piston} - P_{rod \ end} \left(A_{piston} - A_{rod} \right) = F_{est. \ load \ on \ cyl.}$

$P_{blank \ end} \times \dfrac{\pi}{4} \left(0.203^2 \right) - 345{,}000 \times \dfrac{\pi}{4} \left(0.203^2 - 0.102^2 \right) = 178{,}000$

Thus $P_{blank \ end} = 5{,}758{,}000 \text{ Pa} = 5758 \text{ kPa}$

Pump Output Power = $(5758 + 517 + 27.6) \times (0.00247)$
$= 15.6 \text{ kW}$

$$\text{Pump Input Power} = \frac{\text{Pump Output Power}}{\eta_v \, \eta_m} = \frac{15.6}{0.92 \times 0.90}$$

$$= \underline{18.8 \text{ kW}}$$

(c) Pump Input Power = T N

where $N = 1800 \dfrac{\text{rev}}{\text{min}} \times \dfrac{1 \text{ min}}{60 \text{ s}} \times \dfrac{2\pi \text{ rad}}{1 \text{ rev}} = 188 \text{ rad}/_{\text{s}}$

$18{,}800 = T \times 188$ Thus $T = \underline{100\,\text{N} \bullet \text{m}}$

(d) Power delivered to load = $F_{\text{load}} \, V_{\text{cyl ext.}}$

= 178,000 x 0.0762 = 13,600 W = 13.6 kW

Percent of pump input power delivered to load

$= \dfrac{13.6}{18.8} \times 100 = \underline{72.3\,\%}$

6-69. The computer program is written as follows:

```
PRINT "Computer Analysis of Hydraulic System in Fig. 6-42"
INPUT "Enter the Cylinder Piston Diameter(in):", CYLPD
INPUT "Enter the Cylinder Rod Diameter(in):", CYLRD
INPUT "Enter the Extending Speed of Cylinder(in/s):", VCYL
INPUT "Enter the External Load on Cylinder(lb):", FCYL
INPUT "Enter the Pump Volumetric Efficiency(%):", PVOLEFF
INPUT "Enter the Pump Mechanical Efficiency(%):", PMEFF
INPUT "Enter the Pump Speed(rpm):", PSPD
INPUT "Enter the Pump Inlet Pressure(psig):", PINP
INPUT "Enter Press Drop in Pump Disch Line(psi):", DPFWDL
INPUT "Enter Press Drop in Tank Return Line(psi):", DPRTRL

APIST = 3.14 * CYLPD ^ 2 / 4
AROD = 3.14 * CYLRD ^ 2 / 4
QPACT = APIST * VCYL * 60 / 231
QPTHEOR = QPACT / (PVOLEFF / 100)
VOLDISP = 231 * QPTHEOR / PSPD
PBLKEND = (FCYL + DPRTRL * (APIST - AROD)) / APIST
HPPOUT = (PBLKEND + DPFWDL - PINP) * QPACT / 1714
HPPIN = HPPOUT / (PVOLEFF * PMEFF / 10000)
INTORQ = HPPIN * 63000 / PSPD
HPTOLOAD = FCYL * VCYL / 6600
PCTPTOLD = (HPTOLOAD / HPPIN) * 100

PRINT "The Vol. Displ. Of the Pump is"; VOLDISP; "in³"
```

```
PRINT "Input HP Reqr. to Drive the Pump is"; HPPIN; "HP"
PRINT "Input Torq Reqr to Drive Pump is"; INTORQ; "in•lb"
PRINT "% of Pump Input Power Delivered is"; PCTPTOLD; "%"
END
```

The following are the results of executing the computer program for the three different values of external load on the cylinder:

External Load on Cylinder(lb)	30,000	40,000	50,000
Vol. Displ. Of Pump (in^3)	5.46	5.46	5.46
HP Reqr to Drive Pump(HP)	19.7	25.2	30.7
Torq Reqr to Drive Pump(in• lb)	689	881	1073
% of Pump In Prw Deliv to Load(%)	69.3	72.2	74.1

6-70.   Computer Project.

CHAPTER 7   FLUID POWER ACTUATORS

7-1.   A single acting cylinder can exert a force in only the extending direction. Single acting cylinders do not retract hydraulically. Retraction is accomplished by using gravity or by the inclusion of a compression spring in the rod end. Double acting cylinders can be extended and retracted hydraulically.

7-2.   1. Flange mount.
        2. Trunnion mount.
        3. Clevis mount.
        4. Foot and centerline lug mounts.

7-3.   Some cylinders contain cylinder cushions at the ends of the cylinder to slow the piston down near the ends of the stroke. This prevents excessive impact when the piston is stopped by the end caps as illustrated in Figure 7-7.

7-4.   A double-rod cylinder is one in which the rod extends out of the cylinder at both ends. Since the force and speed are the same for either end, this type of cylinder is typically used when the same task is to be performed at either end.

7-5.   Telescoping rod cylinders contain multiple cylinders which slide inside each other. They are used where long work strokes are required but the full retraction length must be minimized.

7-6.   A limited rotation hydraulic actuator provides rotary output motion over a finite angle. A hydraulic motor is an actuator which can rotate continuously.

7-7.   Simple design and subsequent low cost.

7-8.   Since vane motors are hydraulically balanced, they are fixed displacement units.

7-9.   The vanes must have some means other than centrifugal force to hold them against the cam ring. Some designs use springs while other types use pressure-loaded vanes.

7-10.   Yes and either fixed or variable displacement units can be used.

7-11. 1. Volumetric efficiency equals the theoretical flow rate
          the motor should consume, divided by the actual flow
          rate consumed by the motor.
       2. Mechanical efficiency equals the actual torque
          delivered by the motor divided by the torque the motor
          should theoretically deliver.
       3. Overall efficiency equals the actual power delivered
          by the motor divided by the actual power delivered to
          the motor.

7-12. A motor uses more flow than it theoretically should
       because the motor inlet pressure is greater than the motor
       discharge pressure. Thus, leakage flow passes through a
       motor from the inlet port to the discharge port.

7-13. A hydrostatic transmission is a system consisting of a
       hydraulic pump, a hydraulic motor and appropriate valves
       and pipes, which can be used to provide adjustable speed
       drives for many practical applications. Four advantages of
       hydrostatic transmissions are:

       1. Infinitely variable speed and torque in either
          direction and over the full speed and torque range.
       2. Extremely high power per weight ratio.
       3. Can be stalled without damage.
       4. Low inertia of rotating members permits fast starting
          and stopping with smoothness and precision.

7-14. An electro-hydraulic stepping motor is a device which uses
       a small electrical stepping motor to control the huge
       power available from a hydraulic motor. The electro-
       hydraulic stepping motor consists of three components:

       1. Electrical stepping motor.
       2. Hydraulic servo-valve.
       3. Hydraulic motor.

       The electrical stepping motor (See Figure 7-37) rotates a
       precise, fixed amount per each electrical pulse received.
       This motor is directly coupled to the rotary linear
       translator of the servo-valve. The flow forces, in the
       servo-valve, are directly proportional to the rate of flow
       through the valve. The speed and direction of rotation of
       the hydraulic motor reproduces the motion of the electric
       motor and the servo-valve provides feedback through
       mechanical linkage.

7-15. The theoretical torque output is proportional to inlet pressure and volumetric displacement which is independent of motor speed.

7-16. The effective cylinder area is not the same for the extension and retraction strokes. This is due to the effect of the piston rod.

7-17. Single acting cylinders are retracted by gravity or by the inclusion of a compression spring in the rod end of the cylinder.

7-18. True since $T_A = T_T \eta_m = \dfrac{V_D P}{6.28} \times \eta_m$

7-19. Linear actuator: flow rate and piston diameter.
Rotary actuator: flow rate and volumetric displacement.

7-20. The speed and volumetric displacement requirements of the motoring unit (hydraulic cylinder or motor).

7-21. Displacement is the volume of oil required to produce one revolution of the motor. Torque rating is the torque delivered by the motor at rated pressure.

7-22. Some designs use springs, whereas other types use pressure-loaded vanes.

7-23. Pressure exerts a force on the pistons. The piston thrust is transmitted to the angled swash plate causing torque to be created in the drive shaft.

7-24. An increase in the working load results in an increase in volumetric displacement. This decreases motor speed for a constant pump flow rate.

7-25. Piston motor.

7-26. By using the following equation:

$$Q_{actual} = \frac{Q_{theoretical}}{\eta_V} = \frac{V_D N}{231 \, \eta_V}$$

7-27. A first class lever is characterized by the lever fixed hinge pin located between the cylinder and load rod pins. In a second class lever, the load rod pin is located between the fixed hinge pin and cylinder rod pin. For a

87

third class lever, the cylinder rod pin lies in between the load rod pin and the fixed hinge pin.

7-28. A moment is the product a force and its moment arm relative to a given point.

7-29. A moment arm is the perpendicular distance from a given point to the line of action of a force.

7-30. The cylinder is clevis mounted to allow the rod pinned end to travel along the circular path of the lever as it rotates about its fixed hinge pin.

7-31. A torque is the product of a force and its torque arm relative to a given axis of rotation. The torque arm is the distance from the axis of rotation measured perpendicular to the line of action of the force.

Thus for example, for the first class lever of Figure 7-14, the axis of rotation is the fixed hinge pin centerline. The load torque that the cylinder must overcome thus equals the produce of the load force F_{load} and its torque arm $L_2 \cos \theta$ relative to the hinge pin axis of rotation.

Hence a torque arm is a force's distance to an axis of rotation and a moment arm is a force's distance to a point. Hence a moment tends to bend a member about a point whereas a torque tends to rotate a member about an axis.

7-32. (a) $\text{Pressure} = \dfrac{\text{force(lb)}}{\text{piston area}(\text{in}^2)} = \dfrac{1200}{\dfrac{\pi}{4} \times 1.5^2} = \dfrac{1200}{1.767} = \underline{679 \text{ psi}}$

(b) $\text{Velocity} = \dfrac{\text{input flow}\left(\text{ft}^3/\text{s}\right)}{\text{piston area}(\text{ft}^2)} = \dfrac{25/448}{\dfrac{\pi}{4} \times 1.5^2 / 144} = \dfrac{0.0558}{0.0123}$

$= \underline{4.54 \text{ ft/s}}$

(c) $\text{HP} = \dfrac{4.54 \, \text{ft}/\text{s} \times 1200 \text{ lb}}{550} = \underline{9.91 \text{ HP}}$

(d) $\text{Pressure} = \dfrac{\text{force (lb)}}{\text{piston area}(\text{in}^2) - \text{rod area}(\text{in}^2)}$

$$= \frac{1200}{1.767 - \frac{\pi}{4} \times 0.75^2} = \frac{1200}{1.33} = \underline{902 \text{ psi}}$$

(e) Velocity $= \dfrac{\text{input flow}\left(ft^3/_s\right)}{\text{piston area}\left(ft^2\right) - \text{rod area}\left(ft^2\right)}$

$$= \frac{0.0558}{1.33/144} = \underline{6.04 \ ft/_s}$$

(f) $HP = \dfrac{6.04 \ ft/_s \times 1200 \text{ lb}}{550} = \underline{13.18 \text{ HP}}$

7-33. (a) $P = \dfrac{F}{A} = \dfrac{5000}{\dfrac{\pi}{4} \times 0.040^2} = \underline{3.98 \text{ MPa}}$

(b) $v = \dfrac{Q}{A} = \dfrac{0.0016}{\dfrac{\pi}{4} \times 0.040^2} = \underline{1.27 \ m/_s}$

(c) $kW = PQ = 3980 \text{ kPa} \times 0.0016 \ m^3/_s = \underline{6.37 \text{ kW}}$

(d) $P = \dfrac{5000}{\dfrac{\pi}{4}\left(0.040^2 - 0.020^2\right)} = \underline{5.31 \text{ MPa}}$

(e) $v = \dfrac{0.0016}{\dfrac{\pi}{4}\left(0.040^2 - 0.020^2\right)} = \underline{1.70 \ m/_s}$

(f) $kW = 5310 \times 0.0016 = \underline{8.50 \text{ kW}}$

7-34. $v\left(\dfrac{in}{min}\right) = \dfrac{Q\left(\dfrac{gal}{min}\right) \times \dfrac{231 \text{ in}^3}{1 \text{ gal}}}{A\left(in^2\right)}$ Hence $C_1 = \underline{231}$

$v\left(\dfrac{m}{s}\right) = \dfrac{Q\left(\dfrac{m^3}{s}\right)}{A\left(m^2\right)}$ Hence $C_2 = \underline{1}$

7 − 35. $F_{ext} - F_{ret} = P A_P - P\left(A_P - A_R\right) = P A_P - P\left(A_P - \dfrac{A_P}{4}\right)$

$$= P A_P - \dfrac{3}{4} P A_P = \dfrac{1}{4} P A_P$$

Therefore the difference = $\dfrac{1}{4}$ × pressure × piston area

7-36. There would be a net force to extend the cylinder. This net force would have the following value which is the same as that obtained in Exercise 7-35.

$F_{net\ extending} = \dfrac{1}{4}$ × pressure × piston area

7-37. First, calculate the steady state piston velocity (V) prior to deceleration.

$$V = \dfrac{Q_{pump}}{A_{piston}} = \dfrac{\left(\dfrac{20}{448}\right) \dfrac{ft^3}{s}}{\left(\dfrac{\dfrac{\pi}{4} \times 2^2}{144}\right) ft^2} = \dfrac{0.0446}{0.0218} = 2.05\ \dfrac{ft}{s}$$

Next, calculate the deceleration (a) of the piston during the 1 inch displacement (S) using the constant acceleration (or deceleration) equation.

$$a = \dfrac{V^2}{2 S} = \dfrac{\left(2.05\ \dfrac{ft}{s}\right)^2}{2 \times \dfrac{1}{12}\ ft} = 25.2\ \dfrac{ft}{s^2}$$

Substituting into Newton's Law of Motion Equation yields:

$$P_2 \left(A_{piston} - A_{cushion\ plunger}\right) + \mu W - P_1 A_{piston} = \dfrac{W}{g} a$$

Solving for P_2 yields a usable equation.

$$P_2 = \dfrac{\dfrac{W a}{g} + P_1 A_{piston} - \mu W}{A_{piston} - A_{cushion\ plunger}}$$

Substituting known values produces the desired result.

$$P_2 = \frac{1000 \times 25.2 \big/ 32.2 + 500 \times \dfrac{\pi}{4} \times 2^2 - 0.15 \times 1000}{\dfrac{\pi}{4} \times 2^2 - \dfrac{\pi}{4} 0.75^2}$$

$$P_2 = \frac{783 + 1571 - 150}{3.14 - 0.442} = \frac{2204}{2.70} = \underline{816 \text{ psi}}$$

7-38. The following metric data are applicable:

Pump flow $= 20 \text{ gpm} = 0.0000632 \times 20 = 0.00126 \text{ m}^3\!/\!_s$

Hydr. cyl. dia. $= 2 \text{ in} = 2 \text{ in} \times \dfrac{1 \text{ ft}}{12 \text{ in}} \times \dfrac{1 \text{ m}}{3.28 \text{ ft}} = 0.0508 \text{ m}$

Cushion plunger dia. $= 0.75 \text{ in} \times \dfrac{1 \text{ ft}}{12 \text{ in}} \times \dfrac{1 \text{ m}}{3.28 \text{ ft}} = 0.0191 \text{ m}$

Cushion plunger length $= 1 \text{ in} \times \dfrac{1 \text{ ft}}{12 \text{ in}} \times \dfrac{1 \text{ m}}{3.28 \text{ ft}} = 0.0254 \text{ m}$

Weight of cylinder load $= 1000 \text{ lb} \times \dfrac{1 \text{ N}}{0.225 \text{ lb}} = 4440 \text{ N}$

Coefficient of friction $= 0.15$

Pump pressure relief valve setting $= 500 \text{ psi} \times \dfrac{1 \text{ Pa}}{0.000145 \text{ psi}}$

$$= 3450 \text{ kPa}$$

We now first calculate the steady state piston velocity (V) prior to deceleration.

$$V = \frac{Q_{pump}}{A_{piston}} = \frac{0.00126 \text{ m}^3\!/\!_s}{\dfrac{\pi}{4} \times 0.0508^2 \text{ m}^2} = 0.622 \text{ m}\!/\!_s$$

Next we calculate the acceleration (a) of the piston during the 0.0254m displacement using the constant acceleration (or deceleration) equation.

91

$$a = \frac{V^2}{2S} = \frac{\left(0.622 \frac{m}{s}\right)^2}{2 \times 0.0254 \text{ m}} = 7.62 \frac{m}{s^2}$$

Substituting into Newton's Law of Motion Equation and solving for P_2 yields:

$$P_2 = \frac{\frac{W a}{g} + P_1 A_{piston} - \mu W}{A_{piston} - A_{cushion\ plunger}}$$

Substituting known values produces the desired result.

$$P_2 = \frac{\frac{4440 \times 7.62}{9.81} + 3{,}450{,}000 \times \frac{\pi}{4} \times 0.0508^2 - 0.15 \times 4440}{\frac{\pi}{4} \times 0.0508^2 - \frac{\pi}{4} \times 0.0191^2}$$

$$P_2 = \frac{3450 + 6990 - 666}{0.00203 - 0.000287} = \frac{9774}{0.001743} = \underline{5610 \text{ kPa}}$$

7-39. $L_1 = L_2 = 10 \text{ in} \times \frac{2.54 \text{ cm}}{1 \text{ in}} = 25.4 \text{ cm}$

$\phi = 0°$, $F_{load} = 1000 \text{ lb} \times \frac{1 \text{ N}}{0.225 \text{ lb}} = 4444 \text{ N}$

(a) First Class Lever:

$$F_{cyl} = \frac{L_2}{L_1 \cos \phi} \times F_{load} = \frac{25.4}{25.4 \times 1} \times 4444 = \underline{4444 \text{ N}}$$

Second Class Lever:

$$F_{cyl} = \frac{L_2}{\left(L_1 + L_2\right) \cos \phi} \times F_{load} = \frac{25.4 \times 4444}{(25.4 + 25.4) \times 1} = \underline{2222 \text{ N}}$$

Third Class Lever:

$$F_{cyl} = \frac{L_1 + L_2}{L_2 \cos \phi} \times F_{load} = \frac{25.4 + 25.4}{25.4 \times 1} \times 4444 = \underline{8888 \text{ N}}$$

(b) Repeat part (a) with $\theta = 10°$

<u>Answers are the same as those given in part (a).</u>

(c) Repeat part (a) with $\phi = 5°$ and $20°$

First Class Lever:

$$F_{cyl}\left(\phi = 5°\right) = \frac{4444}{\cos 5°} = \underline{4461\ N}$$

$$F_{cyl}\left(\phi = 20°\right) = \frac{4444}{\cos 20°} = \underline{4729\ N}$$

Second Class Lever:

$$F_{cyl}\left(\phi = 5°\right) = \frac{2222}{\cos 5°} = \underline{2231\ N}$$

$$F_{cyl}\left(\phi = 20°\right) = \frac{2222}{\cos 20°} = \underline{2365\ N}$$

Third Class Lever:

$$F_{cyl}\left(\phi = 5°\right) = \frac{8888}{\cos 5°} = \underline{8922\ N}$$

$$F_{cyl}\left(\phi = 20°\right) = \frac{8888}{\cos 20°} = \underline{9458\ N}$$

7-40.   Equating moments about fixed pin C yields:

$$F_{cyl} \times 400\ mm = F_{load} \times 500\ mm$$

$$F_{cyl} = \frac{500}{400} \times F_{load} = 1.25 \times 1000\ N = \underline{1250\ N}$$

7-41.   Equating moments about fixed pin A due to the cylinder force F and the 1000 lb weight yields:

2000 x perpend. dist. AG = F x perpend. dist. AE

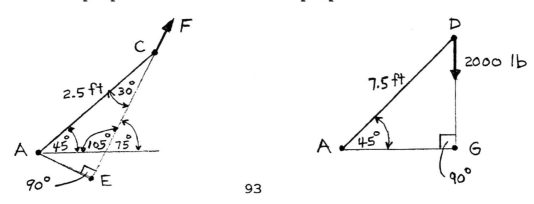

From trigonometry of right triangles we have:

$$\cos 45° = \frac{AG}{7.5} \quad \text{Thus} \quad AG = 7.5 \cos 45° = 5.30 \, \text{ft}$$

$$\sin 30° = \frac{AE}{2.5} \quad \text{Thus} \quad AE = 2.5 \sin 30° = 1.25 \, \text{ft}$$

$$2000 \times 5.30 = F \times 1.25 \quad \text{Hence} \quad F = \underline{8480 \, \text{lb}}$$

7-42. Setting the sum of the forces on pin C equal to zero (from Newton's Law of Motion, $F = ma = 0$ since $a = 0$ for constant velocity motion) yields the following for the X and Y axes:

Y axis: $F_{BC} \sin 60° - F_{BD} \sin 60° = 0 \quad$ Thus $\quad F_{BC} = F_{BD}$

X axis: $F_{cyl} - F_{BC} \cos 60° - F_{BD} \cos 60° = 0$

Thus $F_{cyl} - 2 F_{BC} \cos 60° = 0 \quad$ or $\quad F_{BC} = \dfrac{F_{cyl}}{2 \cos 60°}$

Similarly setting the sum of forces on pin C equal to zero for the Y axis direction yields:

$F_{BC} \sin 60° - F_{load} = 0 \quad$ Therefore we have:

$$F_{load} = F_{BC} \sin 60° = \frac{\sin 60°}{2 \cos 60°} \times F_{cyl} = \frac{\tan 60°}{2} \times 1000 = \underline{866 \, \text{lb}}$$

7-43. First, solve for the volumetric displacement.

$$V_D = \pi \left(1.25^2 - 0.4^2\right) \times 0.75 = 3.31 \, \text{in}^3$$

Then solve for the pressure that must be developed to overcome the load.

$$P = \frac{6.28 \, T}{V_D} = \frac{6.28 \times 750}{3.31} = \underline{1423 \, \text{psi}}$$

7-44. $V_D = \pi \left(R_V^2 - R_R^2\right) L = \pi \left(0.032^2 - 0.010^2\right) \times 0.020 = 58.1 \times 10^{-6} \, \text{m}^3$

$$P = \frac{6.28\ T}{V_D} = \frac{6.28 \times 85}{58.1 \times 10^{-6}} = \underline{9.19\ MPa}$$

7-45. (a) $N = \dfrac{231\ Q}{V_D} = \dfrac{231 \times 15}{6} = \underline{577.5\ rpm}$

(b) $T = \dfrac{V_D\ P}{6.28} = \dfrac{6 \times 2000}{6.28} = \underline{1911\ in \bullet lb}$

(c) $HP = \dfrac{T\ N}{63,000} = \dfrac{1911 \times 577.5}{63,000} = \underline{17.5\ HP}$

7-46. (a) $N = \dfrac{Q}{V_D} = \dfrac{0.001\ {}^{m^3}\!/\!{}_s}{100 \times 10^{-6}\ {}^{m^3}\!/\!{}_{rev}} = 10\ {}^{rev}\!/\!{}_s = \underline{600\ rpm}$

(b) $T = \dfrac{V_D\ P}{6.28} = \dfrac{(100 \times 10^{-6}) \times (140 \times 10^5)}{6.28} = \underline{222.9\ N \bullet m}$

(c) Power $= T\ N = (222.9) \times (10 \times 2\pi) = 14,000\ W = \underline{14.0\ kW}$

7-47. Equations are: $Q = \dfrac{V_D\ N}{231}$, $T = \dfrac{P\ V_D}{6.28}$ and $HP = \dfrac{T\ N}{63,000}$

Thus $V_D = \dfrac{6.28\ T}{P} = \dfrac{6.28 \times (10 \times 1000)}{1000} = 62.8\ in^3$

and $Q = \dfrac{6.28 \times 30}{231} = \underline{8.16\ gpm}$

and $HP = \dfrac{(10 \times 1000) \times 30}{63,000} = \underline{4.76\ HP}$

7-48. $Q = V_D\ N$ and $T = \dfrac{P\ V_D}{6.28}$

So $V_D = \dfrac{6.28\ T}{P} = \dfrac{6.28\ (0.3 \times 4000)}{1 \times 10^8} = 0.0000754\ m^3 = 0.0754\ L$

$Q = V_D\ N = \dfrac{0.0000754 \times 30}{60} = \underline{0.0000377\ {}^{m^3}\!/\!{}_s}$

$$\text{Power} = P\left(\frac{N}{m^2}\right) \times Q\left(\frac{m^3}{s}\right) = \left(1 \times 10^8\right) \times 0.0000377 = \underline{3.77 \text{ kW}}$$

7-49. $$HP = \frac{(\Delta P)Q}{1714} = \frac{1600 \times 100}{1714} = \underline{93.3 \text{ HP}}$$

7-50. The metric data are as follows:

$$\text{Pump disch arg e pressure} = 2000 \text{ psi} \times \frac{1 \text{ kPa}}{0.145 \text{ psi}} = 13{,}800 \text{ kPa}$$

$$\text{Pump flow} = 100 \text{ gpm} = 0.0000632 \times 100 = 0.00632 \, \frac{m^3}{s}$$

$$\text{Pr essure at motor inlet} = 1800 \text{ psi} \times \frac{1 \text{ kPa}}{0.145 \text{ psi}} = 12{,}400 \text{ kPa}$$

$$\text{Motor disch arg e pressure} = 200 \text{ psi} \times \frac{1 \text{ kPa}}{0.145 \text{ psi}} = 1380 \text{ kPa}$$

$$\text{Power} = (\Delta P)Q = (12{,}400 - 1{,}380) \text{ kPa} \times 0.00632 \, \frac{m^3}{s} = \underline{69.6 \text{ kW}}$$

7-51. Friction

7-52. Friction

7-53. $$HP = \frac{TN}{63{,}000} \quad \text{so} \quad T = \frac{63{,}000 \times HP}{N} = \frac{63{,}000 \times 4}{1750} = \underline{144 \text{ in} \bullet \text{lb}}$$

7-54. (a) $$T = \frac{P V_D}{6.28}$$

Since P and V_D are both constant, torque T remains constant. This would, however, double the HP per the following equation:

$$HP = \frac{TN}{63{,}000}$$

(b) Torque T remains constant while the HP is cut in half.

7-55. (a) First, calculate the theoretical flow rate.

$$Q_T = \frac{V_D \, N}{231} = \frac{8 \times 2000}{231} = 69.3 \text{ gpm}$$

$$\eta_v = \frac{Q_T}{Q_A} \times 100 = \frac{69.3}{75} \times 100 = \underline{92.4 \%}$$

(b) To find η_m, we need to calculate the theoretical torque.

$$T_T = \frac{V_D \, P}{6.28} = \frac{8 \times 1500}{6.28} = 1911 \text{ in} \bullet \text{lb}$$

$$\eta_m = \frac{T_A}{T_T} \times 100 = \frac{1800}{1911} \times 100 = \underline{94.2 \%}$$

(c) $\eta_o = \dfrac{\eta_v \, \eta_m}{100} = \dfrac{92.4 \times 94.2}{100} = \underline{87.0 \%}$

(d) $\text{HP} = \dfrac{T_A \, N}{63,000} = \dfrac{1800 \times 2000}{63,000} = \underline{57.1 \text{ HP}}$

7-56. (a) $Q_T = V_D N = \left(130 \times 10^{-6} \dfrac{\text{m}^3}{\text{rev}}\right) \times \left(\dfrac{2000}{60} \dfrac{\text{rev}}{\text{s}}\right) = 0.00433 \dfrac{\text{m}^3}{\text{s}}$

$$\eta_v = \frac{Q_T}{Q_A} \times 100 = \frac{0.00433}{0.005} \times 100 = \underline{86.6 \%}$$

(b) $T_T = \dfrac{V_D N}{6.28} = \dfrac{\left(130 \times 10^{-6}\right) \times \left(105 \times 10^5\right)}{6.28} = 217.4 \text{ N} \bullet \text{m}$

$$\eta_m = \frac{T_A}{T_T} \times 100 = \frac{200}{217.4} \times 100 = \underline{92.0 \%}$$

(c) $\eta_o = \dfrac{\eta_v \, \eta_m}{100} = \dfrac{86.6 \times 92.0}{100} = \underline{79.7 \%}$

(d) $\text{Power} = T_A N = 200 \times \left(\dfrac{2000}{60} \times 2 \pi\right) = 41,900 \text{ W} = \underline{41.9 \text{ kW}}$

7-57. $\eta_o = \dfrac{T_A N / 63,000}{P Q_A / 1714} \times 100 = \dfrac{1300 \times 1750 / 63,000}{1000 \times 75 / 1714} \times 100 = \underline{82.4 \%}$

7-58. $T_{theor} = \dfrac{P\,V_D}{6.28} = T_{act}$ if $\eta_m = 100\%$ and

$Q_{theor} = \dfrac{V_D N}{231} = Q_{act}$ if $\eta_v = 100\%$

Thus for $\eta_v = 100\%$ we have:

$\dfrac{Q_{act}}{N} = \dfrac{V_D}{231} = 0.075$, So $V_D = \underline{17.3 \text{ in}^3}$

For $\eta_m = 100\%$ we have: $T_{act} = \dfrac{3000 \times 17.3}{6.28} = \underline{8260 \text{ in} \bullet \text{lb}}$

Note that the calculated values of V_D and T are theoretical values. Actual values can be calculated as follows:

Since a motor consumes more flow than it theoretically should we have: $V_{D\,act} = \eta_v V_{D\,theor}$

Similarly since a motor produces less torque than it theoretically should we have: $T_{act} = \eta_m T_{theor}$

Hence we need values of η_v and η_m to obtain actual values of V_D and T.

A relationship in terms of overall efficiency can be developed as follows:

$V_{D\,act} T_{act} = \eta_m \eta_v V_{D\,theor} T_{theor} = \eta_o V_{D\,theor} T_{theor}$

But this equation alone does not allow for the calculation of $V_{D\,act}$ and T_{act} even if the value of η_o is given.

7-59. (a) Pump theoretical flowrate $= \dfrac{\text{displ. of pump} \times \text{pump speed}}{231}$

$= \dfrac{6 \times 100}{231} = 26.0 \text{ gpm}$

Pump act. flowrate = pump theor. flowrate x pump vol. eff.

$$= 26.0 \times 0.85 = 22.1 \text{ gpm}$$

Motor theor flowrate = pump act flowrate x motor vol. eff.

$$= 22.1 \times 0.94 = 20.8 \text{ gpm}$$

$$\text{Motor displacement} = \frac{\text{motor theoretical flowrate} \times 231}{\text{motor speed}}$$

$$= \frac{20.8 \times 231}{600} = 8.01 \text{ in}^3$$

(b) $HP_{\text{del to motor}} = \dfrac{\text{system pressure} \times \text{actual flowrate to motor}}{1714}$

$$= \frac{1500 \times 22.1}{1714} = 19.3 \text{ HP}$$

$$HP_{\text{del by motor}} = 19.3 \times 0.94 \times 0.92 = 16.7 \text{ HP}$$

$$\text{Torque delivered by motor} = \frac{\text{HP delivered by motor} \times 63,000}{\text{motor speed}}$$

$$= \frac{16.7 \times 63,000}{600} = 1756 \text{ in} \bullet \text{lb}$$

7-60. (a) $Q_{TP} = V_{DP}N_{P} = \left(100 \times 10^{-6}\right) \times \dfrac{1000}{60} = 0.00167 \text{ } ^{m^3}\!/_{s}$

$$Q_{AP} = Q_{TP}\eta_{VP} = 0.00167 \times 0.85 = 0.00142 \text{ } ^{m^3}\!/_{s}$$

$$Q_{TM} = Q_{AP}\eta_{VM} = 0.00142 \times 0.94 = 0.00133 \text{ } ^{m^3}\!/_{s}$$

$$V_{DM} = \frac{Q_{TM}}{N_{M}} = \frac{0.00133}{600\!/_{60}} = 0.000133 \text{ m}^3 = 133 \text{ cm}^3$$

(b) $Power_{\text{act to motor}} = P Q_{AM} = \left(105 \times 10^5\right) \times 0.00142 = 14,900 \text{ W}$

$$Power_{\text{act by motor}} = 14,900 \times 0.94 \times 0.92 = 12,900 \text{ W}$$

$$T_{\text{act by motor}} = \frac{12,900}{600 \times 2\pi\!/_{60}} = 205 \text{ N} \bullet \text{m}$$

7-61. The computer program is written as follows:

```
PRINT "Comput Analy of Hydrostat Transm of Exercise 7-59"
INPUT "Enter the Pump Volume Displacement (in³):", PUMPVD
INPUT "Enter the Pump Volumetric Efficiency(%):", PVOLEFF
INPUT "Enter the Pump Mechanical Efficiency(%):", PMEFF
INPUT "Enter the Pump Speed(rpm):", PSPD
INPUT "Enter the Motor Volumetric Efficiency(%):", MVOLEFF
INPUT "Enter the Motor Mechanical Efficiency(%):", MMEFF
INPUT "Enter the Motor Speed(rpm):", MSPD
INPUT "Enter the System Pressure(psi):", SYSPRESS

QPTHEOR = PUMPVD * PSPD / 231
QPACT = QPTHEOR * PVOLEFF / 100
QMTHEOR = QPACT * MVOLEFF / 100
MOTORVD = QMTHEOR * 231 / MSPD
HPTOMOT = SYSPRESS * QPACT / 1714
HPBYMOT = HPTOMOT * MVOLEFF * MMEFF / (100 * 100)
TORBYMOT = HPBYMOT * 63000 / MSPD

PRINT "The Volume Displ. of Motor is"; MOTORVD; "in³"
PRINT "The Motor Output Torque is"; TORBYMOT; "in • lb"
END
```

The following are the results of executing the computer
program for the three different values of operating
pressure:

Operating pressure (psi)	1000	1500	2000
Volume Displ. of Motor(in³)	7.99	7.99	7.99
Motor Output Torque(in • lb)	1170	1754	2339

7-62. Computer Project

100

CHAPTER 8   CONTROL COMPONENTS IN HYDRAULIC SYSTEMS

8-1.   Directional control valves determine the path through which a fluid traverses within a given circuit.

8-2.   A check valve is a directional control valve which permits free flow in one direction and prevents any flow in the opposite direction.

8-3.   A pilot check valve always permits free flow in one direction, but permits flow in the normally blocked opposite direction only if pilot pressure is applied at the pilot pressure port of the valve.

8-4.   A four-way directional control valve is one which has four different ports.

8-5.   This valve contains a spool which can be actuated into three different functioning positions. The center position is obtained by the action of the springs alone.

8-6.   1. Manually
        2. Air piloted
        3. Solenoid actuated

8-7.   A solenoid is an electric coil. When the coil is energized, it creates a magnetic force that pulls the armature into the coil. This causes the armature to push on the push rod to move the spool of the valve.

8-8.   The open-center type connects all ports together when the valve is unactuated. The closed-center design has all ports blocked when the valve is unactuated.

8-9.   A shuttle valve is another type of directional control valve. It permits a system to operate from either of two fluid power sources. One application is for safety in the event that the main pump can no longer provide hydraulic power to operate emergency devices.

8-10.   To limit the maximum pressure experienced in a hydraulic system.

8-11.   A pressure reducing valve is another type of pressure control valve. It is used to maintain reduced pressures in specified locations of hydraulic systems.

8-12. An unloading valve is used to permit a pump to build up to an adjustable pressure setting and then allow it to discharge to the tank at essentially zero pressure as long as pilot pressure is maintained on the valve from a remote source.

8-13. A sequence valve is a pressure control device. Its purpose is to cause a hydraulic system to operate in a pressure sequence.

8-14. To maintain control of a vertical cylinder so that it does not descend due to gravity.

8-15. Flow control valves are used to regulate the speed of hydraulic cylinders and motors by controlling the flow rate to these actuators.

8-16. A pressure compensated flow control valve is one which provides the desired flow rate regardless of changes in system pressure.

8-17. A servo valve is a directional control valve which has infinitely variable positioning capability. Servo valves are coupled with feedback sensing devices which allow for the vary accurate control of position, velocity and acceleration of an actuator.

8-18. Mechanical-hydraulic servo valves use only mechanical components. Electrical-hydraulic servo valves typically use an electrical torque motor, a double-nozzle pilot stage and a sliding spool second stage.

8-19. See Figure 8-46 for a block diagram of a closed-loop system.

8-20. A hydraulic fuse prevents hydraulic pressure from exceeding an allowable value in order to protect circuit components from damage. It is analogous to an electric fuse.

8-21. A pressure switch is an instrument that automatically senses a change in pressure and opens or closes an electrical switching element when a predetermined pressure point is reached. Four types are diaphragm, bourdon tube, sealed piston and dia-seal piston.

8-22. A temperature switch is an instrument that automatically senses a change in temperature and opens or closes an

electrical switching element when a predetermined
temperature point in reached.

8-23.   A normally open switch is one in which no current can flow
        through the switching element until the switch is
        actuated. In a normally closed switch, current flows
        through the switching element until the switch is
        actuated.

8-24.   A shock absorber is a device which brings a moving load to
        a gentle rest through the use of metered hydraulic fluid.
        Two applications are moving cranes and automotive
        suspension systems.

8-25.   In the design of Figure 8-4, the check valve poppet has
        the pilot piston attached to the threaded poppet stem by a
        nut. The light spring holds the poppet seated in a no-flow
        condition by pushing against the pilot piston. The purpose
        of the separate drain port is to prevent oil from creating
        a pressure buildup on the bottom of the piston.

8-26.   Pilot check valves are frequently used for locking
        hydraulic cylinders in position.

8-27.   Flow can go through the valve in four unique ways
        depending on the spool position.

        (a) Spool Position 1: Flow can go from P to A and B to T.
        (b) Spool Position 2: Flow can go from A to T and P to B.

8-28.   1. Low handle load and no sudden surges.
        2. Can take higher velocities and more flow than a spool
           valve of the same pipe size.

8-29.   A compound pressure relief valve (See Figure 8-20) is one
        which operates in two stages. Referring to Figure 8-31,
        the operation is as follows:

        In normal operation the balanced piston is in hydraulic
        balance. For pressures less than the valve setting, the
        piston is held on its seat by a light spring. As soon as
        pressure reaches the setting of the adjustable spring, the
        poppet is forced off its seat. This limits the pressure in
        the upper chamber.

        The restricted flow through the orifice and into the upper
        chamber results in an increase in pressure in the lower
        chamber. This causes an imbalance in hydraulic forces

which tends to raise the piston off its seat. When the pressure difference between the upper and lower chambers reaches 20 psi, the large piston lifts off its seat to permit flow directly to tank.

8-30.   Unloading valve: see Figure 8-34.
Sequence valve: see Figure 8-36.

8-31.   This design incorporates a hydrostat which maintains a constant 20 psi differential across the throttle which is an orifice whose area can be adjusted by an external knob setting. The orifice area setting determines the flow rate to be controlled. The hydrostat is held normally open by a light spring.

However, it starts to close as inlet pressure increases and overcomes the light spring force. This closes the opening through the hydrostat and, thereby, blocks off all flow in excess of the throttle setting.

As a result, the only oil that will pass through the valve is the amount which 20 psi can force through the throttle. Flow exceeding this amount can be used by other parts of the circuit or return to the tank via the pressure relief valve.

8-32.   This model can operate with 0.5 to 1600 psi pressures. It has a dia-seal piston directly acting on a snap-action switch. This design combines diaphragm accuracy with piston long life and high proof pressure tolerance. The electrical switching element opens or closes an electrical circuit in response to the actuating force it receives from the pressure sensing element.

8-33.   These shock absorbers are filled completely with oil. Therefore, they may be mounted in any position or at any angle. The spring-return units are entirely self-contained, extremely compact types that require no external hoses, valves or fittings. In this spring-returned type, a built-in cellular accumulator accommodates oil displaced by the piston rod as the rod moves inward.

These shock absorbers are multiple orifice hydraulic devices. When a moving load strikes the bumper of the shock absorber, it sets the rod and piston in motion. The moving piston pushes oil through the series of holes. The resistance to the oil flow caused by the holes, creates a pressure that acts against the piston to oppose the moving load.

8-34.   Two

8-35.   Three

8-36.   A rotary valve consists of a rotor closely fitted in a valve body as shown in Figure 8-22. Passages in the rotor connect or block off the ports in the valve body to provide the desired flow paths.

8-37.   To shift the spool in directional control valves.

8-38.   1. Using non-pressure-compensated flow control valves.
        2. Using pressure-compensated flow control valves.

8-39.   The pressure at which a pressure relief valve begins to open.

8-40.   One port connects to the pressure line from the pump.
        Second port connects to the drain line to the oil tank.

8-41.   Control direction of flow.
        Control flow rate.
        Control pressure.

8-42.   A hydraulic fuse, as in the case of a pressure relief valve, prevents hydraulic pressure from exceeding an allowable value in order to protect circuit components from physical damage. A hydraulic fuse is analogous to an electrical fuse because they both are one-shot devices. On the other hand, a pressure relief valve is analogous to an electrical circuit breaker because they both are resetable devices.

8-43.   Position is the location of the spool inside the valve.
        Way is the flow path through the valve.
        Port is the opening in the valve body for the fluid to enter or exit.

8-44.   A cartridge valve is a valve that is designed to be assembled into a cavity of a ported manifold block (alone or along with other cartridge valves and hydraulic components) in order to perform the valve's intended function.

8-45.   The slip-in design cartridge valve uses a bolted cover
        while a screw-type design uses threads for assembling into
        the manifold block.

8-46.   1. Reduced number of fittings to connect hydraulic lines
           between various components in a system.
        2. Reduced oil leakage and contamination due to fewer
           fittings.
        3. Lower system installation time and costs.
        4. Reduced service time since faulty cartridge valves can
           be easily changed without disconnecting fittings.
        5. Smaller space requirements of overall system.

8-47.   Directional control, pressure relief, pressure reducing,
        unloading and flow control functions.

8-48.   Integrated hydraulic circuits are compact hydraulic
        systems formed by integrating various cartridge valves and
        other components into a single, machined, ported manifold
        block.

8-49. $HP = \dfrac{PQ}{1714} = \dfrac{2000 \times 25}{1714} = \underline{29.2\ HP}$

8-50. $HP = \dfrac{PQ}{1714} = \dfrac{30 \times 25}{1714} = \underline{0.44\ HP}$

8-51. $kW\ Power = PQ = \left(140 \times 10^5\right) \times \left(0.0016 \times 10^{-3}\right) = \underline{22.4\ kW}$

8-52. $kW\ Power = PQ = \left(2 \times 10^5\right) \times \left(0.0016 \times 10^{-3}\right) = \underline{0.32\ kW}$

CHAPTER 9   HYDRAULIC CIRCUIT DESIGN AND ANALYSIS

9-1.   1. Safety of operation.
       2. Performance of desired function.
       3. Efficiency of operation.

9-2.   A regenerative circuit is used to speed up the extending
       speed of a double-acting hydraulic cylinder.

9-3.   The load carrying capacity for a regenerative cylinder
       equals the pressure times the piston rod area rather than
       the pressure times the piston area.

9-4.   Fail-safe circuits are those designed to prevent injury to
       the operator or damage to equipment. In general, they
       prevent the system from accidentally falling on an
       operator and they also prevent overloading of the system.

9-5.   A hydraulic motor may be driving a machine having a large
       inertia. This would create a flywheel effect on the motor
       and stopping the flow of fluid to the motor would cause it
       to act as a pump. The circuit should be designed to
       provide fluid to the motor while it is pumping to prevent
       it from pulling in air.

9-6.   Open circuit hydrostatic transmissions are drives in which
       the pump draws its fluid from a reservoir. Its output is
       then directed to a hydraulic motor and discharged from the
       motor back into the reservoir. In a closed circuit drive,
       exhaust oil from the motor is returned directly to the
       pump inlet.

9-7.   An air-over-oil system is one using both air and oil to
       obtain the advantages of each medium.

9-8.   1. Weight loaded or gravity.
       2. Spring loaded type.
       3. Gas loaded type.

9-9.   1. Piston type: principal advantage is its ability to
          handle very high or low temperature system fluids
          through the utilization of compatible "O" ring seals.

       2. Diaphragm type: primary advantage is its small weight-
          to-volume ratio which makes it suitable almost
          exclusively for air-born applications.

3. Bladder type: greatest advantage is the positive sealing between the gas and oil chambers.

9-10. 1. Auxiliary power source to store oil delivered by the pump during a portion of the work cycle.
       2. Compensator for internal or external leakage during an extended period of time during which the system is pressurized but not in operation.
       3. An emergency power source where a cylinder must be retracted even though the normal supply of oil pressure is lost due to a pump or electrical power failure.
       4. Elimination or reduction of high-pressure pulsations or hydraulic shock.

9-11. A mechanical hydraulic servo system is a closed-loop system using a mechanical feedback. One application is an automotive power steering system.

9-12. One relief valve (nearest pump) protects the system (pump to three-way valve) from over-pressure due to pump flow against a closed three-way valve. The other relief valve (nearest the accumulator) protects the system (rod end of cylinder to check valve and accumulator) from over-pressure while the cylinder is extending.

9-13. Yes. Use a regenerative circuit with a cylinder having a rod area equal to one-half the piston area. Also can use a double rod cylinder having equal area rods at each end.

9-14. Weight-loaded type. Pressure can be changed by changing the magnitude of the dead weight attached to the top of the piston.

9-15. Valve spool moves with the load.
       Valve sleeve moves with the input.

9-16. (a) $v_{P\ ext} = \dfrac{Q_P}{A_r} = \dfrac{25\ \dfrac{gal}{min} \times \dfrac{231\ in^3}{1\ gal} \times \dfrac{1\ min}{60\ s}}{10\ in^2} = \underline{9.63\ in/s}$

$F_{load\ ext} = P\,A_r = 1500\ \dfrac{lb}{in^2} \times 10\ in^2 = \underline{15{,}000\ lb}$

(b) $v_{P\ ret} = \dfrac{Q_P}{A_p - A_r} = \dfrac{25 \times \dfrac{231}{60}}{20 - 10} = \underline{9.63\ in/s}$

$$F_{\text{load ret}} = P\left(A_p - A_r\right) = 1500\,\frac{lb}{in^2} \times 10\,in^2 = \underline{15{,}000\ lb}$$

9-17.   (a) $v_{\text{P ext}} = \dfrac{Q_p}{A_r} = \dfrac{0.0016\,\frac{m^3}{s}}{65 \times 10^{-4}\,m^2} = \underline{0.25\,\frac{m}{s}}$

$$F_{\text{load ext}} = P\,A_r = \left(105 \times 10^5\right) \times \left(65 \times 10^{-4}\right) = \underline{68{,}300\ N}$$

(b) $v_{\text{P ret}} = \dfrac{Q_p}{A_p - A_r} = \dfrac{0.0016}{130 \times 10^{-4} - 65 \times 10^{-4}} = \underline{0.25\,\frac{m}{s}}$

$$F_{\text{load ret}} = P\left(A_p - A_r\right) = \left(105 \times 10^5\right) \times \left(65 \times 10^{-4}\right) = \underline{68{,}300\ N}$$

9-18.   Use the circuit of Figure 9-11 entitled "Hydraulic Cylinder Sequence Circuit". The left cylinder of Figure 9-11 becomes the clamp cylinder of Figure 9-45 and the right cylinder of Figure 9-11 becomes the work cylinder of Figure 9-45.

9-19.   The directional control valve (DCV) should have a center-closed configuration to allow the accumulator to charge when the DCV is in its unactuatad (spring-centered) mode. The existing center bypass configuration does not allow the accumulator to charge when the DCV is unactuated.

9-20.   A check valve is needed in the hydraulic line just upstream from where the pilot line to the unloading valve is connected to the hydraulic line. Otherwise, the unloading valve would behave like a pressure relief valve and thus, valuable energy would be wasted.

9-21.   Cylinder 1 extends, cylinder 2 extends.
Cylinder 1 retracts, cylinder 2 retracts.
Above cycle repeats.

9-22.   Both manually actuated directional control valves must be actuated in order to extend or retract the hydraulic cylinder.

9-23.   Both cylinder strokes would be synchronized.

9-24.   Cylinder 2 will extend through its complete stroke receiving full pump flow while cylinder 1 does not move. As soon as cylinder 2 has extended through its complete stroke, cylinder 1 receives full pump flow and extends through its complete stroke. This is because system pressure builds up until load resistance is overcome to move cylinder 2 with the smaller load.

Then pressure continues to increase until the load on cylinder 1 is overcome. This causes cylinder 1 to then extend. In the retraction mode, the cylinders move in the same sequence.

9-25. $P_1 = \dfrac{F_1 + F_2}{A_{P1}} = \dfrac{5000 + 5000}{10} = \underline{1000 \text{ psi}}$

9-26. For cylinder 1 we have:

$$P_1 A_{P1} - P_2 \left(A_{P1} - A_{R1} \right) = F_1$$

Similarly for cylinder 2 we have:

$$P_2 A_{P2} - P_3 \left(A_{P2} - A_{R2} \right) = F_2$$

Adding both equations and noting that $A_{P2} = A_{P1} - A_{R1}$ yields:

$$P_1 A_{P1} - P_3 \left(A_{P2} - A_{R2} \right) = F_1 + F_2$$

Solving for P_1 gives the desired result.

$$P_1 = \frac{F_1 + F_2 + P_3 \left(A_{P2} - A_{R2} \right)}{A_{P1}} = \frac{5000 + 5000 + 50 \left(8 - 2 \right)}{10}$$

$$= \underline{1030 \text{ psi}}$$

9-27. $P_1 = \dfrac{F_1 + F_2}{A_{P1}} = \dfrac{22{,}000 + 22{,}000}{65 \times 10^{-4}} = \underline{6.77 \text{ MPa}}$

9-28. Using the equation developed in Exercise 9-26 we have:

$$P_1 = \frac{F_1 + F_2 + P_3 \left(A_{P2} - A_{R2} \right)}{A_{P1}}$$

$$P_1 = \cfrac{22{,}000 \text{ N} + 22{,}000 \text{ N} + 300{,}000 \dfrac{\text{N}}{\text{m}^2} \times (50 - 15) \text{ cm}^2 \times \left(\dfrac{1 \text{ m}}{100 \text{ cm}}\right)^2}{65 \text{ cm}^2 \times \left(\dfrac{1 \text{ m}}{100 \text{ cm}}\right)^2}$$

$$= \underline{6.93 \text{ MPa}}$$

9-29. Cylinders 1 and 2 are identical and are connected by identical lines. Therefore they receive equal flows and can sustain equal loads ($F_1 = F_2$). Also

$$Q_4 = \frac{40}{2} = 20 \text{ gpm}, \quad Q_6 = \frac{20(8^2 - 4^2)}{8^2} = 15 \text{ gpm}$$

and $\quad Q_8 = Q_9 = 2(15) = 30 \text{ gpm}$

We have the following useable equations:

$$v = \frac{0.408 \, Q}{D^2}, \quad N_R = \frac{v \, D}{v} \quad \text{and} \quad H_L = \sum\left(f \times \frac{L}{D} + K\right)\frac{v^2}{2g}$$

Solving for velocities yields:

$$v_1 = \frac{0.408 \times 40}{1.5^2} = 7.25 \, \text{ft/s}, \quad v_2 = \frac{0.408 \times 40}{1^2} = 16.3 \, \text{ft/s}$$

$$v_3 = \frac{0.408 \times 40}{1.25^2} = 10.4 \, \text{ft/s}, \quad v_4 = \frac{0.408 \times 20}{1^2} = 8.16 \, \text{ft/s}$$

$$v_6 = \frac{0.408 \times 15}{0.75^2} = 10.9 \, \text{ft/s}, \quad v_8 = v_9 = \frac{0.408 \times 30}{1.25^2} = 7.83 \, \text{ft/s}$$

We can now calculate the Reynolds numbers.

$$N_{R1} = \frac{7.25 \times 1.5/12}{0.001} = 906, \quad N_{R2} = \frac{163. \times 1.0/12}{0.001} = 1358$$

$$N_{R3} = \frac{10.4 \times 1.25/12}{0.001} = 1083, \quad N_{R4} = \frac{8.16 \times 1.0/12}{0.001} = 680$$

$$N_{R6} = \frac{10.9 \times 0.75/12}{0.001} = 681, \quad N_{R8} = N_{R9} = \frac{7.83 \times 1.25/12}{0.001} = 816$$

Since all flows are laminar, $f = \dfrac{64}{N_R}$. Also $\Delta P = \gamma H_L$ Thus

$$H_{L1} = \left(\frac{64}{906} \times \frac{6}{1.5/12} + 0.75 \right) \times \frac{7.25^2}{64.4} = 3.38 \text{ ft} = \frac{50 \times 3.38}{144} \text{ psi}$$

$$= 1.17 \text{ psi}$$

$$H_{L2} = \left(\frac{64}{1358} \times \frac{30}{1.0/12} + 4 \right) \times \frac{16.3^2}{64.4} = 86.5 \text{ ft} = 30.0 \text{ psi}$$

$$H_{L3} = \left(\frac{64}{1083} \times \frac{20}{1.25/12} + 6.8 \right) \times \frac{10.4^2}{64.4} = 30.5 \text{ ft} = 10.6 \text{ psi}$$

$$H_{L4} = \left(\frac{64}{680} \times \frac{10}{1.0/12} + 0 \right) \times \frac{8.16^2}{64.4} = 11.7 \text{ ft} = 4.05 \text{ psi}$$

$$H_{L6} = \left(\frac{64}{681} \times \frac{10}{0.75/12} + 1.8 \right) \times \frac{10.9^2}{64.4} = 31.1 \text{ ft} = 10.8 \text{ psi}$$

$$H_{L8} = H_{L9} = \left(\frac{64}{816} \times \frac{80}{1.25/12} + 5.75 \right) \times \frac{7.83^3}{64.4} = 62.8 \text{ ft} = 21.8 \text{ psi}$$

$$F_1 = F_2 = (1000 - 1.17 - 30.0 - 10.6 - 4.05) \times \frac{\pi}{4}\left(8^2\right)$$

$$- (10.8 + 21.8) \times \frac{\pi}{4}\left(8^2 - 4^2\right) = 47,900 - 1200 = \underline{46,700 \text{ lb}}$$

9-30.   Cylinders 1 and 2 are identical and are connected by identical lines. Therefore they receive equal flows and sustain equal loads $\left(F_1 = F_2\right)$.

We have the following useable equations:

$$v = \frac{Q}{A}, \quad N_R = \frac{vD}{v}, \quad H_L = \sum \left(f \times \frac{L}{D} + K \right) \frac{v^2}{2g}$$

Values of system parameters are as follows:

112

$$\gamma = 50 \frac{lb}{ft^3} \times \frac{1\,N}{0.225\,lb} \times \left(\frac{3.28\,ft}{1\,m}\right)^3 = 7840\ \text{N}/_{m^3}$$

$$\nu = 0.001 \frac{ft^2}{s} \times \left(\frac{1\,m}{3.28\,ft}\right)^2 = 0.0000930\ \text{m}^2/_s$$

Cylinder piston diameter $= 8\,in \times \dfrac{1\,m}{39.4\,in} = 0.203\,m$

Cylinder rod diameter $= \dfrac{4}{39.4} = 0.102\,m$

$L_1 = 1.83\,m,\quad D_1 = 0.0381\,m \qquad L_6 = 3.05\,m,\quad D_6 = 0.0190\,m$

$L_2 = 9.15\,m,\quad D_2 = 0.0254\,m \qquad L_7 = 3.05\,m,\quad D_7 = 0.0190\,m$

$L_3 = 6.10\,m,\quad D_3 = 0.0317\,m \qquad L_8 = 12.2\,m,\quad D_8 = 0.0317\,m$

$L_4 = 3.05\,m,\quad D_4 = 0.0254\,m \qquad L_9 = 12.2\,m,\quad D_9 = 0.0317\,m$

$L_5 = 3.05\,m,\quad D_5 = 0.0254\,m$

$$\Delta P_{pump} = 1000\,psi \times \frac{1\,Pa}{0.000145\,psi} = 6.90\,MPa$$

$$Q_{pump} = 40 \frac{gal}{min} \times \frac{231\,in^3}{1\,gal} \times \left(\frac{1\,m}{39.4\,in}\right)^3 \times \frac{1\,min}{60\,s} = 0.00252\ \text{m}^3/_s$$

$$Q_6 = \frac{0.00252}{2} = 0.00126\ \frac{m^3}{s},\quad Q_4 = 0.00126 \times \frac{8^2}{8^2 - 4^2} = 0.00168\ \frac{m^3}{s}$$

$$Q_3 = Q_9 = 2 \times 0.00168 = 0.00336\ \text{m}^3/_s$$

Solving for velocities yields:

$$v_1 = \frac{0.00252}{\dfrac{\pi}{4} \times 0.0381^2} = 2.21\ \text{m}/_s,\qquad v_2 = \frac{0.00252}{\dfrac{\pi}{4} \times 0.0254^2} = 4.97\ \text{m}/_s$$

$$v_8 = \frac{0.00252}{\frac{\pi}{4} \times 0.0317^2} = 3.19 \, ^m/_s, \qquad v_6 = \frac{0.00126}{\frac{\pi}{4} \times 0.0190^2} = 4.44 \, ^m/_s$$

$$v_4 = \frac{0.00168}{\frac{\pi}{4} \times 0.0254^2} = 3.32 \, ^m/_s, \qquad v_3 = v_9 = \frac{0.00336}{\frac{\pi}{4} \times 0.0317^2} = 4.26 \, ^m/_s$$

We can now solve for the Reynolds numbers.

$$N_{R1} = \frac{2.21 \times 0.0381}{0.0000930} = 905, \qquad N_{R2} = \frac{4.97 \times 0.0254}{0.0000930} = 1357$$

$$N_{R8} = \frac{3.19 \times 0.0317}{0.0000930} = 1087, \qquad N_{R6} = \frac{4.44 \times 0.0190}{0.0000930} = 907$$

$$N_{R4} = \frac{3.32 \times 0.0254}{0.0000930} = 907, \qquad N_{R3} = N_{R9} = \frac{4.26 \times 0.0317}{0.0000930} = 1452$$

Since all flows are laminar, $f = {64}/{N_R}$. Thus we have:

$$H_{L1} = \left(\frac{64}{905} \times \frac{1.83}{0.0381} + 0.75 \right) \times \frac{2.21^2}{19.6} = 1.08 \, m = 7840 \times 1.08 \, Pa$$
$$= 8470 \, Pa$$

$$H_{L2} = \left(\frac{64}{1357} \times \frac{9.15}{0.0254} + 4 \right) \times \frac{4.97^2}{19.6} = 26.5 \, m = 207,000 \, Pa$$

$$H_{L8} = \left(\frac{64}{1087} \times \frac{12.2}{0.0317} + 6.8 \right) \times \frac{3.19^2}{19.6} = 15.3 \, m = 120,000 \, Pa$$

$$H_{L6} = \left(\frac{64}{907} \times \frac{3.05}{0.0190} + 0 \right) \times \frac{4.44^2}{19.6} = 11.4 \, m = 89,300 \, Pa$$

$$H_{L4} = \left(\frac{64}{907} \times \frac{3.05}{0.0254} + 1.8 \right) \times \frac{3.32^2}{19.6} = 5.78 \, m = 45,300 \, Pa$$

$$H_{L3} + H_{L9} = \left(\frac{64}{1452} \times \frac{6.10 + 12.2}{0.0317} + 5.75 \right) \times \frac{4.26^2}{19.6} = 28.9 \, m$$
$$= 226,000 \, Pa$$

114

$$F_1 = F_2 = \left(6.90 \times 10^6 - 8470 - 207{,}000 - 120{,}000 - 89{,}300\right) \times \frac{\pi}{4} \times$$

$$\left(0.203^2 - 0.102^2\right) - \left(45{,}300 + 226{,}000\right) \times \frac{\pi}{4} \times 0.203^2$$

$$F_1 = F_2 = 157{,}000 - 8780 = \underline{148{,}000 \text{ N}}$$

9-31. $\quad HP_{loss} = \dfrac{(\Delta P)\, Q}{1714} \quad$ and $\quad 1 \text{ HP} = 42.4\ \text{BTU}/\text{min} \quad$ Thus

$$HP_{loss} = \frac{(1.1 + 30.0 + 10.6) \times 40}{1714} + \frac{4.05 \times 20}{1714} + \frac{10.8 \times 15}{1714} + \frac{21.8 \times 30}{1714}$$

$$HP_{loss} = 0.97 + 0.05 + 0.09 + 0.38 = 1.49 \text{ HP}$$

Heat generation rate $= 1.49 \times 42.4 = 63.2\ \text{BTU}/\text{min} = \underline{3790\ \text{BTU}/\text{hr}}$

9-32. $\quad v = \dfrac{Q_{cyl}}{A} \quad$ where each cylinder receives one half of pump flow.

$$v_{ext} = \frac{Q_{blank\ end}}{A_{piston}} = \frac{20\ \dfrac{gal}{min} \times \dfrac{231\ in^3}{1\ gal} \times \dfrac{1\ min}{60\ s}}{\dfrac{\pi}{4} \times 8^2\ in^2} = \frac{77\ \dfrac{in^3}{s}}{50.3\ in^2} = \underline{1.53\ \frac{in}{s}}$$

$$v_{ret} = \frac{Q_{rod\ end}}{A_{piston} - A_{rod}} = \frac{77\ in^3\!/s}{\dfrac{\pi}{4}\left(8^2 - 4^2\right)\ in^2} = \underline{2.04\ in\!/s}$$

9-33. $\quad$ Power Loss (Watts) $= \left(\Delta P\right) \dfrac{N}{m^2} \times Q\ \dfrac{m^3}{s}$

$$= (8{,}470 + 207{,}000 + 120{,}000) \times 0.00252$$

$$+ 2 \times 89{,}300 \times 0.00126$$

$$+ 2 \times 45{,}300 \times 0.00168$$

$$+ 226{,}000 \times 0.00336$$

$$= 845 + 225 + 152 + 759$$

$$= 1981 \text{ Watts} = \underline{1.981 \text{ kW}}$$

9-34. $v = \dfrac{Q_{cyl}}{A}$ where each cylinder receives one half of pump flow.

$$V_{ext} = \frac{Q_{blank\ end}}{A_{piston}} = \frac{0.00126 \ ^{m^3}\!/_{s}}{\dfrac{\pi}{4} \times 0.203^2 \ m^2} = \underline{0.0389 \ ^{m}\!/_{s}}$$

$$V_{ret} = \frac{Q_{rod\ end}}{A_{piston} - A_{rod}} = \frac{0.00126 \ ^{m^3}\!/_{s}}{\dfrac{\pi}{4} \times \left(0.203^2 - 0.102^2\right) m^2} = \underline{0.0521 \ ^{m}\!/_{s}}$$

9-35. We have the following useable equations:

$$v = \frac{0.408 \, Q}{D^2} \ , \qquad N_R = \frac{v \, D}{v} \ , \qquad H_L = \sum \left(f \times \frac{L}{D} + K \right) \frac{v^2}{2g} \quad \text{Also}$$

$$\text{Pump Power} = \frac{\Delta P(\text{psi}) \times Q\,(\text{gpm})}{1714} = 0.90 \times 25 = 22.5 \text{ HP}$$

$$\text{Thus} \quad Q_{pump} = \frac{22.5 \times 1714}{1000} = 38.6 \text{ gpm} \qquad \text{Also}$$

$$F_{regenerative} = P_{blank\ end} A_{piston} - P_{rod\ end}\left(A_{piston} - A_{rod}\right)$$

$$Q_1 = Q_{pump} = 38.6 \text{ gpm} \quad \text{and} \quad Q_3 = Q_{pump} + Q_4 \quad \text{Thus we have:}$$

$$A_p V_{P\ ext} = Q_3 = Q_{pump} + \left(A_p - A_r\right) V_{P\ ext} \times \frac{A_p}{A_p}$$

$$\text{Therefore } Q_3 = Q_{pump} + \frac{A_p - A_r}{A_p} Q_3 \quad \text{so} \quad Q_3 = \frac{A_p}{A_r} Q_{pump}$$

$$\text{And} \quad Q_4 = \frac{A_p - A_r}{A_p} \times \frac{A_p}{A_r} Q_{pump} = \frac{A_p - A_r}{A_r} Q_{pump}$$

$$\text{Hence} \quad Q_3 = \frac{^{\pi}\!/_{4} \times 8^2 \times 38.6}{^{\pi}\!/_{4} \times 4^2} = 154 \text{ gpm}$$

116

And $Q_4 = \dfrac{\frac{\pi}{4} \times \left(8^2 - 4^2\right) \times 38.6}{\frac{\pi}{4} \times 4^2} = 116 \text{ gpm}$

Solving for velocities yields:

$v_1 = \dfrac{0.408 \times 38.6}{1.5^2} = 7.00 \text{ ft}/\text{s}$ $v_2 = \dfrac{0.408 \times 38.6}{1^2} = 15.7 \text{ ft}/\text{s}$

$v_3 = \dfrac{0.408 \times 154}{2^2} = 15.7 \text{ ft}/\text{s}$ $v_4 = \dfrac{0.408 \times 116}{1.5^2} = 21.0 \text{ ft}/\text{s}$

We can now calculate the Reynolds numbers.

$N_{R1} = \dfrac{7.00 \times \frac{1.5}{12}}{0.001} = 875$ $N_{R2} = \dfrac{15.7 \times \frac{1.0}{12}}{0.001} = 1308$

$N_{R3} = \dfrac{15.7 \times \frac{2.0}{12}}{0.001} = 2620$ $N_{R4} = \dfrac{21.0 \times \frac{1.5}{12}}{0.001} = 2630$

Since all flows are laminar, $f = \frac{64}{N_R}$. Also $\Delta P = \gamma H_L$

$H_{L1} = \left(\dfrac{64}{875} \times \dfrac{2}{\frac{1.5}{12}} + 10\right) \times \dfrac{7.00^2}{64.4} = 8.50 \text{ ft}$

$= 50 \dfrac{\text{lb}}{\text{ft}^3} \times 8.50 \text{ ft} \times \dfrac{1 \text{ psi}}{144 \frac{\text{lb}}{\text{ft}^2}} = 2.95 \text{ psi}$

$H_{L2} = \left(\dfrac{64}{1308} \times \dfrac{20}{\frac{1.0}{12}} + 5\right) \times \dfrac{15.7^2}{64.4} = 64.1 \text{ ft} = \dfrac{50 \times 64.1}{144} = 22.3 \text{ psi}$

$H_{L3} = \left(\dfrac{64}{2620} \times \dfrac{30}{\frac{2}{12}} + 0.75\right) \times \dfrac{15.7^2}{64.4} = 19.7 \text{ ft} = \dfrac{50 \times 19.7}{144} = 6.84 \text{ psi}$

$H_{L4} = \left(\dfrac{64}{2630} \times \dfrac{30}{\frac{1.5}{12}} + 0.75\right) \times \dfrac{21.0^2}{64.4} = 45.1 \text{ ft}$

$= \dfrac{50 \times 45.1}{144} = 15.7 \text{ psi}$

117

$$F = (1000 - 2.95 - 22.3 - 6.84) \times \frac{\pi}{4} \times 8^2$$

$$- (1000 - 2.95 - 22.3 + 15.7) \times \frac{\pi}{4} \times (8^2 - 4^2)$$

Thus $F = 48,700 - 37,300 = \underline{11,400 \text{ lb}}$

9-36.   Metric data is as follows:

<u>Electric Motor:</u>   Power $= 25 \text{ HP} \times \dfrac{0.746 \text{ kW}}{1 \text{ HP}} = 18.65 \text{ kW}$

Overall efficiency = 90%

<u>Pump:</u> Disch arg e pressure $= 1000 \text{ psi} \times \dfrac{1 \text{ kPa}}{0.145 \text{ psi}} = 6897 \text{ kPa}$

<u>Oil:</u> Kin. Visc. $= v = 0.001 \dfrac{\text{ft}^2}{\text{s}} \times \left(\dfrac{1 \text{ m}}{3.28 \text{ ft}}\right)^2 = 0.0000930 \; \text{m}^2\!/\text{s}$

Weight Dens. $= \gamma\left(\dfrac{\text{N}}{\text{m}^3}\right) = 157 \times \gamma\left(\dfrac{\text{lb}}{\text{ft}^3}\right) = 157 \times 50 = 7850 \dfrac{\text{N}}{\text{m}^3}$

<u>Cylinder:</u> Piston Diameter $= 8 \text{ in} \times \dfrac{1 \text{ ft}}{12 \text{ in}} \times \dfrac{1 \text{ m}}{3.28 \text{ ft}} = 0.203 \text{ m}$

Rod Diameter = 4 in = 0.102 m

Elbows: K factor = 0.75

Pipes:

No.	Length (m)	Dia. (m)
1	0.61	0.0381
2	6.10	0.0254
3	9.15	0.0508
4	9.15	0.0381
5	6.10	0.0254

We have the following useable equations:

$$v = \frac{Q}{A} \; , \qquad N_R = \frac{v\,D}{v} \; , \qquad \sum\left(f \times \frac{L}{D} + K\right) \times \frac{v^2}{2g}$$

$$\text{Pump Power} = \Delta P(kPa) \times Q\left(\frac{m^3}{s}\right) = 0.90 \times 18.65 = 16.79 \text{ kW}$$

$$Q_{pump} = \frac{16.79 \text{ kW}}{6897 \text{ kPa}} = 0.00243 \text{ }^{m^3}\!/\!_s$$

$$F_{regen} = P_{blank\,end}A_{piston} - P_{rod\,end}\left(A_{piston} - A_{rod}\right)$$

$$Q_1 = Q_2 = Q_{pump} = 0.00243 \text{ }^{m^3}\!/\!_s$$

Per the solution to Exercise 9-35, we have the following two equations to solve for the flow rates in lines 3 and 4:

$$Q_3 = \frac{A_P}{A_r}Q_{pump} = \frac{\pi\!/\!_4 \times 8^2 \times 0.00243}{\pi\!/\!_4 \times 4^2} = 0.00972 \text{ }^{m^3}\!/\!_s$$

$$Q_4 = \frac{A_P - A_r}{A_r}Q_{pump} = \frac{\pi\!/\!_4 \times \left(8^2 - 4^2\right) \times 0.00243}{\pi\!/\!_4 \times 4^2} = 0.00729 \text{ }^{m^3}\!/\!_s$$

Solving for the velocities yields:

$$v_1 = \frac{Q_1}{A_1} = \frac{0.00243}{\frac{\pi}{4} \times 0.0381^2} = 2.13 \text{ }^m\!/\!_s \qquad v_2 = \frac{0.00243}{\frac{\pi}{4} \times 0.0254^2} = 4.80 \text{ }^m\!/\!_s$$

$$v_3 = \frac{0.00972}{\frac{\pi}{4} \times 0.0508^2} = 4.80 \text{ }^m\!/\!_s \qquad v_4 = \frac{0.00729}{\frac{\pi}{4} \times 0.0381^2} = 6.39 \text{ }^m\!/\!_s$$

We can now calculate the Reynolds numbers.

$$N_{R1} = \frac{3.13 \times 0.0381}{0.0000930} = 873 \qquad N_{R2} = \frac{4.80 \times 0.0254}{0.0000930} = 1311$$

$$N_{R3} = \frac{4.80 \times 0.0508}{0.0000930} = 2620 \qquad N_{R4} = \frac{6.39 \times 0.0381}{0.0000930} = 2620$$

Since all flows are la min ar, $f = \dfrac{64}{N_R}$, Also $\Delta P = \gamma H_L$

$$H_{L1} = \left(\frac{64}{873} \times \frac{0.610}{0.0381} + 10 \right) \times \frac{2.13^2}{19.6} = 2.58 \text{ m} = 2.58 \times 7850$$
$$= 20{,}300 \text{ Pa}$$

$$H_{L2} = \left(\frac{64}{1311} \times \frac{6.10}{0.0254} + 5 \right) \times \frac{4.80^2}{19.6} = 19.63 \text{ m} = 154{,}000 \text{ Pa}$$

$$H_{L3} = \left(\frac{64}{2620} \times \frac{9.15}{0.0508} + 0.75 \right) \times \frac{4.80^2}{19.6} = 6.05 \text{ m} = 47{,}500 \text{ Pa}$$

$$H_{L4} = \left(\frac{64}{2620} \times \frac{9.15}{0.0381} + 0.75 \right) \times \frac{6.39^2}{19.6} = 13.8 \text{ m} = 108{,}000 \text{ Pa}$$

$$F(kN) = \left(6897 \text{ kPa} - 20.3 - 154 - 47.5 \right) \times \frac{\pi}{4} \times 0.203^2$$
$$- \left(6897 \text{ kPa} - 20.3 - 154 + 108 \right) \times \frac{\pi}{4} \times \left(0.203^2 - 0.102^2 \right)$$

$$F = 216 - 165 = \underline{51 \text{ kN}}$$

9-37.   HP Loss $= \sum Q(\Delta P) =$ Pipe 1 Loss + Pump Loss + Pipe 2 Loss
+ Pipe 3 Loss + Pipe 4 Loss

$$= \frac{38.6 \times 2.95}{1714} + (25 - 22.5) + \frac{38.6 \times 22.3}{1714}$$

$$+ \frac{154 \times 6.84}{1714} + \frac{116 \times 15.7}{1714}$$

HP Loss $= 0.07 + 2.50 + 0.50 + 0.61 + 1.06 = \underline{4.74 \text{ HP}}$

9-38.   Power Loss $= \sum Q(\Delta P)$ kW

$=$ Pipe 1 Loss + Pump Loss + Pipe 2 Loss

+ Pipe 3 Loss + Pipe 4 Loss

$= 0.00243 \times 20.3 + (18.7 - 16.8)$

$+ 0.00243 \times 154 + 0.00972 \times 47.5$

$+ 0.00729 \times 108$

$$= 0.049 + 1.90 + 0.374 + 0.46 + 0.79$$

$$\text{Power Loss = Heat Generation Rate} = \underline{3.57 \text{ kW}}$$

9-39. Per the solution to Exercise 9-35, we have Q_{pump} = 38.6 gpm

Upper Position of DCV:

$$v_{ext} = \frac{Q_{pump}}{A_p} = \frac{38.6 \frac{\text{gal}}{\text{min}} \times \frac{231 \text{ in}^3}{1 \text{ gal}} \times \frac{1 \text{ min}}{60 \text{ s}}}{\frac{\pi}{4} \times 8^2 \text{ in}^2} = \frac{149 \frac{\text{in}^3}{\text{s}}}{50.3 \text{ in}^2} = \underline{2.96 \text{ in}/\text{s}}$$

Spring-Centered Position of DCV:

$$v_{ext} = \frac{Q_{pump}}{A_r} = \frac{149}{\frac{\pi}{4} \times 4^2} = \frac{149}{12.6} = \underline{11.8 \text{ in}/\text{s}}$$

Lower Position of DCV:

$$v_{ret} = \frac{Q_{pump}}{A_p - A_r} = \frac{149}{50.3 - 12.6} = \frac{149}{37.7} = \underline{3.95 \text{ in}/\text{s}}$$

9-40. Per solution of Exercise 9-36, we have $Q_{pump} = 0.00243 \text{ m}^3/\text{s}$.

Upper Position of DCV:

$$v_{ext} = \frac{Q_{pump}}{A_p} = \frac{0.00243}{\frac{\pi}{4} \times 0.203^2} = \underline{0.0751 \text{ m}/\text{s}}$$

Spring-Centered Position of DCV:

$$v_{ext} = \frac{Q_{pump}}{A_r} = \frac{0.00243}{\frac{\pi}{4} \times 0.102^2} = \underline{0.297 \text{ m}/\text{s}}$$

Lower Position of DCV:

$$v_{ret} = \frac{Q_{pump}}{A_p - A_r} = \frac{0.00243}{\frac{\pi}{4} \times \left(0.203^2 - 0.102^2\right)} = \underline{0.100 \text{ m}/\text{s}}$$

9-41. The following is the computer program:

```
PRINT "Computer Analysis of Hydraulic System of Exercise 9-29"
INPUT "Enter the Pressure Increase Across Pump(psi):", DLTPPUMP
INPUT "Enter the pump Flowrate(gpm):", QPUMP

INPUT "Enter the Kinematic Viscosity of Oil(ft²/s):", KINVISC

INPUT "Enter the Density of the Oil(lb/ft³):", DENSITY
INPUT "Enter the Cylinder Piston Diameter(in):", PISTDIA
INPUT "Enter the Cylinder Rod Diameter(in):", RODDIA
INPUT "Enter the Diameter of Pipe 1(in):", D1
INPUT "Enter the Diameter of Pipe 2(in):", D2
Input "Enter the Diameter of Pipe 3(in):", D3
INPUT "Enter the Diameter of Pipe 4(in):", D4
INPUT "Enter the Diameter of Pipe 6(in):", D6
INPUT "Enter the Diameter of Pipe 8(in):", D8
INPUT "Enter the Diameter of Pipe 9(in):", D9


Q1 = QPUMP
Q2 = Q1
Q3 = Q1
Q4 = Q1 / 2
APIST = 3.14 * PISTDIA ^ 2 / 4
AROD = 3.14 * RODDIA ^ 2 / 4
Q6 = Q4 * (APIST - AROD) / APIST
Q8 = 2 * Q6
Q9 = Q8


V1 = .408 * Q1 / 1.5 ^ 2
V2 = .408 * Q2 / 1 ^ 2
V3 = .408 * Q3 / 1.25 ^ 2
V4 = .408 * Q4 / 1 ^ 2
V6 = .408 * Q6 / .75 ^ 2
V8 = .408 * Q8 / 1.25 ^ 2
V9 = V8


NR1 = V1 * D1 / (.001 * 12)
NR2 = V2 * D2 / (.001 * 12)
NR3 = V3 * D3 / (.001 * 12)
NR4 = V4 * D4 / (.001 * 12)
NR6 = V6 * D6 / (.001 * 12)
NR8 = V8 * D8 / (.001 * 12)
NR9 = V9 * D9 / (.001 * 12)
```

```
HL1 = ((64 * 6/(NR1 *D1/12)) + .75) * (V1 ^ 2/64.4) * 50/144
HL2 = ((64 * 30/(NR2 * D2/12)) + 4 * (V2 ^ 2/64.4) * 50/144
HL3 = ((64 * 20/(NR3 * D3/12)) + 6.8) * (V3 ^ 2/64.4) * 50/144
HL4 = (64 * 10/(NR4 * D4/12)) * (V4 ^ 2/64.4) * 50/144
HL6 = ((64 * 10/(NR6 * D6/12)) + 1.8) * (V6 ^ 2/64.4) * 50/144
HL8 = ((64 * 40/(NR8 * D8/12)) + 5.75) * (V8 ^ 2/64.4) * 50/144
HL9 = HL8

F1 = (DLTPPUMP-HL1-HL2-HL3-HL4)*APIST-(HL6+HL8+HL9)*(APIST-AROD)
F2 = F1

PRINT "The External Load Cylinder 1 Can Sustain is "; F1; "lb"
PRINT "The External Load Cylinder 2 Can Sustain is "; F2; "lb"

END
```

The following are the results of executing the computer program for the five different pressure increase values across the pump.

Press Inc Acr Pump(psi)	800	900	1000	1100	1200
Ext Load Cyl 1 Sust(lb)	36,600	41,600	46,600	51,700	56,700
Ext Load Cyl 2 Sust(lb)	36,600	41,600	46,600	51,700	56,700

9-42. Computer Project

CHAPTER 10   PNEUMATICS - AIR PREPARATION AND COMPONENTS

10-1.   1. Liquids exhibit greater inertia than do gases.
         2. Liquids exhibit greater viscosity than do gases.
         3. Hydraulic systems require special reservoirs and no-
            leak design components.

10-2.   1. Boyle's Law states that, if the temperature of a given
            amount of gas is held constant, the volume of the gas
            will change inversely with the absolute pressure of
            the gas.
         2. Charles' Law states that, if the pressure on a given
            amount of gas is held constant, the volume of the gas
            will change in direct proportion to the absolute
            temperature.
         3. Gay-Lussac's Law states that, if the volume of a
            given gas is held constant, the pressure exerted by
            the gas is directly proportional to its absolute
            temperature.

10-3.   1. Piston type.
         2. Screw type.
         3. Sliding vane type.

10-4.   Compressors having more than one cylinder are called
         multistage compressors. Staging means dividing the total
         pressure increase among two or more cylinders by feeding
         the exhaust from one cylinder into the inlet of the next
         cylinder. This improves pumping efficiency.

10-5.   The function of an air filter is to remove contaminants
         from the air before it reaches pneumatic components such
         as valves and actuators.

10-6.   An air pressure regulator is used so that a constant
         pressure is available for a given pneumatic system.

10-7.   A lubricator insures proper lubricating of internal
         moving parts of pneumatic components.

10-8.   A pneumatic indicator is a device which provides a two-
         color, two-position visual indication of air pressure.

10-9.   A pneumatic exhaust silencer (muffler) is used to control
         the noise caused by a rapidly exhausting air stream
         flowing into the atmosphere.

10-10. An aftercooler is installed in the airline immediately downstream of the compressor. Compressors do not remove moisture. Thus, an aftercooler is essential to reduce the air temperature to convenient levels and to act as a first stage in removal of moisture prior to entering an air dryer.

Aftercoolers remove only about 80% of the moisture from the air leaving the compressor. An air dryer removes virtually all moisture by lowering the temperature of the pressurized air to a dew point of 50°F.

10-11. Pneumatic actuators are of lighter construction making extensive use of aluminum and other non-ferrous alloys to reduce weight, improve heat transfer characteristics and minimize corrosive action of air.

10-12. 1. Determine pressure capacity requirement.
2. Establish number of stages required.
3. Determine scfm of air required.
4. Size the air receiver and compressor.
5. Determine type of compressor (piston, vane or screw).
6. Establish type of unloader control and pressure settings.

10-13. 1. Supply air at system steady flow rate requirements.
2. Supply air at essentially constant pressure.
3. Dampen pressure pulses either coming from the compressor or the pneumatic system during valve shifting and component operation.
4. Handle transient air demands exceeding compressor capability with a maximum and minimum pressure range.

10-14. Starting torque is the torque produced under load at zero speed.

10-15. Flow capacity constant is the proportionality constant between flow rate and valve pressure drop and downstream pressure. Thus for the same valve pressure drop and downstream pressure, the flow rate increases directly with the flow capacity constant. Hence a large flow capacity constant indicates a large size valve.

10-16. $V_1 = 20\,\text{in}^3$, $P_1 = 30 + 14.7 = 44.7\,\text{psia}$

$$V_2 = 20 - \frac{\pi}{4} \times 2^2 \times 5 = 4.29\,\text{in}^3$$

From Boyle's Law, we have:

$$\frac{20}{4.29} = \frac{P_2}{44.7} \qquad \text{Thus } P_2 = 208.4\,\text{psia} = \underline{193.7\,\text{psig}}$$

10-17. $T_1 = 80 + 460 = 540°\,R$, $T_2 = 150 + 460 = 610°\,R$, $V_1 = 20\,\text{in}^3$

From Charles' Law, we have:

$$\frac{20}{V_2} = \frac{540}{610} \qquad \text{Thus } V_2 = \underline{25.6\,\text{in}^3}$$

10-18. $P_1 = 30 + 14.7 = 44.7\,\text{psia}$

$T_1 = 80 + 460 = 540°\,R$, $T_2 = 160 + 460 = 620°\,R$

Using Gay-Lussac's Law, we obtain:

$$\frac{44.7}{P_2} = \frac{540}{620} \qquad \text{Thus } P_2 = 51.3\,\text{psia} = \underline{36.6\,\text{psig}}$$

10-19. Solve the general gas law for P_2 and substitute known values:

$$P_2 = \frac{P_1 V_1 T_2}{V_2 T_1} = \frac{(1200 + 14.7) \times 2000 \times (250 + 460)}{150 \times (120 + 460)} = 19{,}826\,\text{psia}$$

$$= \underline{19{,}811\,\text{psig}}$$

10-20. $\dfrac{V_1}{V_2} = \dfrac{P_2}{P_1}$ \qquad where \quad $V_1 = 300\,\text{cm}^3$

$$V_2 = 300 - \frac{\pi}{4} \times 5^2 \times 13 = 300 - 255 = 45\,\text{cm}^3$$

$$P_1 = 2 \times 10^5 + 1 \times 10^5 = 3 \times 10^5\,\text{Pa abs}$$

$$\frac{300}{45} = \frac{P_2}{3 \times 10^5}$$

Thus $P_2 = 20 \times 10^5$ Pa abs = 20 bars abs = <u>19 bars gage</u>

10-21. $T_1 = 30 + 273 = 303°$ K   and $T_2 = 65 + 273 = 338°$ K

$$\frac{V_1}{V_2} = \frac{T_1}{T_2} \quad \text{so} \quad \frac{130}{V_2} = \frac{303}{338} \quad \text{and} \quad V_2 = \underline{145 \text{ cm}^3}$$

10-22. $\dfrac{P_1}{P_2} = \dfrac{T_1}{T_2}$ where $P_1 = 2 + 1 = 3$ bars abs

Also $T_1 = 25 + 273 = 298°$ K   and $T_2 = 70 + 273 = 343°$ K

Thus $\dfrac{3}{P_2} = \dfrac{298}{343}$ and $P_2 = 3.45$ bars abs = <u>2.45 bars gage</u>

10-23. $P_2 = \dfrac{P_1 V_1 T_2}{V_2 T_1} = \dfrac{81 \times 1290 \times (120 + 273)}{1000 \times (50 + 273)} = 127$ bars abs

$$= \underline{126 \text{ bars gage}}$$

10-24. $°C = \dfrac{°F - 32}{1.8} = \dfrac{160 - 32}{1.8} = \underline{71.1 °C}$

$°R = °F + 460 = 160 + 460 = \underline{620 °R}$

$°K = °C + 273 = 71.1 + 273 = \underline{344.1 °K}$

10-25. Solve Equation 10-6 for V_1 and let subscript 1 represent atmospheric conditions.

$$V_1 = \frac{V_2 P_2 T_1}{P_1 T_2} = \text{cfm of free air}$$

$$V_1 = \frac{30 \times (150 + 14.7) \times (80 + 460)}{14.7 \times (100 + 460)} = \underline{324 \text{ cfm of free air}}$$

10-26. (a) $V_r = \dfrac{14.7 \, t \left(Q_r - Q_c\right)}{P_{max} - P_{min}} = \dfrac{14.7 \times 10 \times (30 - 0)}{120 - 100} = \underline{221 \text{ ft}^3}$

(b) $V_r = \dfrac{14.7 \times 10 \times (30 - 6)}{120 - 100} = \underline{176 \text{ ft}^3}$

10-27. $V_1 = \dfrac{V_2 P_2 T_1}{P_1 T_2} = \dfrac{1 \times (1000 + 101) \times (20 + 273)}{101 \times (40 + 273)} = \underline{10.2 \text{ std } {}^{m^3}\!/_{min}}$

10-28. **(a)** Consumption rate $= 30 \text{ scfm} \times \left(\dfrac{1 \text{ m}}{3.28 \text{ ft}}\right)^3 = 0.850 \text{ std } {}^{m^3}\!/_{min}$

$$P_{max} = 120 \text{ psi} \times \dfrac{1 \text{ kPa}}{0.145 \text{ psi}} = 828 \text{ kPa}$$

$$P_{min} = 100 \text{ psi} \times \dfrac{1 \text{ kPa}}{0.145 \text{ psi}} = 690 \text{ kPa}$$

$$V_r = \dfrac{101\, t \left(Q_r - Q_c\right)}{P_{max} - P_{min}} = \dfrac{101 \times 10\,(0.850 - 0)}{828 - 690} = \underline{6.22 \text{ m}^3}$$

(b) Compressor delivery rate $= 6 \text{ scfm} \times \left(\dfrac{1 \text{ m}}{3.28 \text{ ft}}\right)^3$

$$= 0.170 \text{ std } {}^{m^3}\!/_{min}$$

$$V_r = \dfrac{101 \times 10\,(0.850 - 0.170)}{828 - 690} = \underline{4.98 \text{ m}^3}$$

10-29. Theoretical HP $= \dfrac{P_{in} Q}{65.4}\left[\left(\dfrac{P_{out}}{P_{in}}\right)^{0.286} - 1\right]$

$$= \dfrac{14.7 \times 200}{65.4}\left[\left(\dfrac{134.7}{14.7}\right)^{0.286} - 1\right] = \underline{39.8 \text{ HP}}$$

Actual HP $= \dfrac{HP_{Theor}}{\eta_o} = \dfrac{39.8}{0.72} = \underline{55.3 \text{ HP}}$

10-30. Theoretical Power (kW) $=$ Actual Power (kW) $\times \eta_o$

$$= \dfrac{P_{in} Q}{17.1}\left[\left(\dfrac{P_{out}}{P_{in}}\right)^{0.286} - 1\right]$$

Substituting known values yields:

$$20 \times 0.75 = \frac{100 \times 4}{17.1} \left[\left(\frac{P_{out}}{100} \right)^{0.286} - 1 \right]$$

Thus $\left(\dfrac{P_{out}}{100} \right)^{0.286} = 0.641 + 1 = 1.641$

And $\dfrac{P_{out}}{100} = 5.66$ so $\underline{P_{out} = 566 \text{ kPa abs}}$

10-31. $T = 100 + 460 = 560° \text{ R}$

$P_1 = 125 + 14.7 = 139.7 \text{ psia}$

$P_2 = 0.53 \times 139.7 = 74.0 \text{ psia}$

Substituting directly into Eqn. 10-9 yields the answer.

$$Q = 22.67 \times 7 \sqrt{\frac{(139.7 - 74.0) \times 74.0}{560}} = \underline{468 \text{ scfm}}$$

10-32. $\dfrac{\text{Downstream pressure}}{\text{Upstream pressure}} = \dfrac{P_2}{P_1} = \dfrac{180 \text{ kPa abs}}{400 \text{ kPa abs}} = 0.45$

Since $\dfrac{P_2}{P_1}$ is less than 0.53, $\underline{\text{the valve is choked}}$.

10-33. $P_1V_1 = P_2V_2$ where state 1 is the standard air state and constant temperature has been assumed.

$$V_2 = \frac{\dfrac{\pi}{4} \times 2.5^2 \times 12 \times 30}{1728} = 1.02 \text{ } ft^3\!\big/\!_{min} \text{ consumed by cyl at 100 psi}$$

Therefore $V_1 = \dfrac{P_2V_2}{P_1} = \dfrac{100 \times 1.02}{14.7} = \underline{6.95 \text{ scfm}}$

10-34. $P_1V_1 = P_2V_2$ where state 1 is the standard air state and constant temperature has been assumed.

$$V_2 = \frac{\pi}{4} \times 0.06^2 \times 0.30 \times 30 = 0.0254 \; \text{m}^3\!/\text{min} \text{ consumed by the cyl}$$

at 700 kPa.

Therefore $V_1 = \dfrac{P_2 V_2}{P_1} = \dfrac{700 \times 0.0254}{100} = \underline{0.178 \;\; \text{std} \; \text{m}^3\!/\text{min}}$

10-35. Ignoring the effect of the rod and assuming constant temperature we have:

$$V_2 = \frac{\pi}{4} \times 0.050^2 \times (0.025 \times 2) \times 80 = 0.00785 \; \text{m}^3\!/\text{min} \text{ consumed by}$$

the cylinder at 600 kPa.

$\dfrac{V_1}{t} = \dfrac{P_2 V_2}{P_1}$ so $t = \dfrac{P_1 V_1}{P_2 V_2} = \dfrac{100 \times 100}{600 \times 0.00785} = 2120 \; s = \underline{35.4 \; \text{min}}$

10-36. $V_2 = \dfrac{\dfrac{\pi}{4} \times 2^2 \times (12 \times 2) \times 200}{1728} = 8.72 \; \text{ft}^3\!/\text{min}$ consumed by the

cylinder at 100 psi.

Thus $V_1 = \dfrac{P_2 V_2}{P_1} = \dfrac{100 \times 8.72}{14.7} = \underline{59.3 \; \text{scfm}}$

10-37. $P_1 V_1 = P_2 V_2$ where state 1 is the standard air state and

constant temperature has been assumed.

$$V_2 = 4 \; \frac{\text{in}^3}{\text{rev}} \times 1750 \; \frac{\text{rev}}{\text{min}} \times \frac{1 \; \text{ft}^3}{1728 \; \text{in}^3} = 4.05 \; \text{ft}^3\!/\text{min} \quad \text{consumed by}$$

the air motor at 100 psi.

Thus $V_1 = \dfrac{P_2 V_2}{P_1} = \dfrac{100 \times 4.05}{14.7} = \underline{27.6 \; \text{scfm}}$

10-38. $P_1 V_1 = P_2 V_2$ where state 1 is the standard air state and

constant temperature has been assumed.

$$V_2 = 0.000080 \ \frac{m^3}{rev} \times 1750 \ \frac{rev}{min} = 0.14 \ m^3\!/min \quad \text{consumed by the}$$

air motor at 700 kPa gage.

$$V_1 = \frac{P_2 V_2}{P_1} = \frac{801 \times 0.14}{101} = \underline{1.11 \ std \ m^3\!/min}$$

$$\text{Power (kW)} = \left(\Delta P\right) \times Q = 700 \ kPa \times \frac{0.14 \ m^3}{60 \ s} = \underline{1.63 \ kW}$$

10-39. (a) $V = \dfrac{\pi}{4} \times 1^2 \times 2 = \underline{1.57 \ in^3}$

(b) $V = \underline{1.57 \ in^3}$

(c) $S = \dfrac{1.57}{\dfrac{\pi}{4} \times 1.5^2} = \underline{0.89 \ in}$

(d) $V = \dfrac{\pi}{4} \times 8^2 \times 2 = \underline{101 \ in^3}$

(e) $Q = 1.57 \times 1 = 1.57 \ \dfrac{in^3}{s} = 94.2 \ \dfrac{in^3}{min} = \underline{0.41 \ gpm}$

(f) $P_{oil} = \dfrac{12,000}{\dfrac{\pi}{4} \times 1.5^2} = 6790 \ psi \quad \text{and} \quad P_{air} = \dfrac{6790}{8^2} = 106 \ psi$

$$Q = 101 \ \frac{in^3}{s} \times \frac{106}{14.7} = 728 \ in^3\!/s \ \text{of std air}$$

$$Q = \frac{728 \times 60}{1728} = \underline{25.3 \ scfm}$$

10-40. The load $= 12,000 \ lb \times \dfrac{1 \ N}{0.225 \ lb} = \underline{53,300 \ N}$

Hydr. cyl. dia. $= 1.5 \ in \times \dfrac{1 \ ft}{12 \ in} \times \dfrac{1 \ m}{3.28 \ ft} = \underline{0.0381 \ m}$

$$\text{Air piston diameter} = 8 \text{ in} \times \frac{1 \text{ ft}}{12 \text{ in}} \times \frac{1 \text{ m}}{3.28 \text{ ft}} = 0.203 \text{ m}$$

$$\text{Oil piston diameter} = 1 \text{ in} \times \frac{1 \text{ ft}}{12 \text{ in}} \times \frac{1 \text{ m}}{3.28 \text{ ft}} = 0.0254 \text{ m}$$

$$\text{Intensifier stroke} = 2 \text{ in} \times \frac{1 \text{ ft}}{12 \text{ in}} \times \frac{1 \text{ m}}{3.28 \text{ ft}} = 0.0508 \text{ m}$$

Intensifier frequency = 1 stroke/s

(a) $V = \dfrac{\pi}{4} \times 0.0254^2 \times 0.0508 = 0.0000257 \text{ m}^3 = \underline{0.0257 \text{ L}}$

(b) $V = \underline{0.0257 \text{ L}}$

(c) $S = \dfrac{0.0000257}{\dfrac{\pi}{4} \times 0.0381^2} = 0.0225 \text{ m} = \underline{22.5 \text{ mm}}$

(d) $V = \dfrac{\pi}{4} \times 0.203^2 \times 0.0508 = 0.00164 \text{ m}^3 = \underline{1.64 \text{ L}}$

(e) $Q = 0.0257 \text{ L} \times \dfrac{1}{\text{s}} = \underline{0.0257 \text{ L}/\text{s}}$

(f) $P_{oil} = \dfrac{53{,}300 \text{ N}}{\dfrac{\pi}{4} \times 0.0381^2} = 46.8 \text{ MPa}$

$$P_{air} = \frac{46.8 \text{ MPa}}{\left(\dfrac{8}{1}\right)^2} = 0.731 \text{ MPa} = 731 \text{ kPa}$$

$$Q = 0.00164 \frac{\text{m}^3}{\text{s}} \times \frac{60 \text{ s}}{1 \text{ min}} \times \frac{731}{101} = \underline{0.712 \text{ std m}^3/\text{min}}$$

10-41. The computer program is written as follows:

```
PRINT "Computer Anal. of Air-Hydr. Intensifier of Exercise 10-39"
INPUT "Enter the Hydraulic Cylinder Load(N):", CYLLOAD
INPUT "Enter the Hydraulic Cylinder Diameter(m):", CYLDIA
INPUT "Enter the Air Piston Diameter(m):", AIRPIDIA
```

```
INPUT "Enter the Oil Piston Diameter(m):", OILPIDIA
INPUT "Enter the Intensifier Stroke(m):", INTSTROK
INPUT "Enter the Intensifier Frequency(strokes/s):", INTFREQ

OILPIA = 3.14 * OILPIDIA ^ 2 / 4
VOLOILP = OILPIA * INSTROK
VOLCYL = VOLOILP
HYDCYLA = 3.14 * CYLDIA ^ 2 / 4
SHYDCYL = VOLCYL / HYDCYLA
AIRCYLA = 3.14 * AIRPIDIA ^ 2 / 4
VOLAIRCY = AIRCYLA * INTSTROK
QOILINT = VOLOILP
POIL = CYLLOAD / HYDCYLA
PAIR = POIL / (8 ^ 2)
QAIRINT = VOLAIRCY * 60 * PAIR / 101000

PRINT "Vol. Displ. of Intensifier Oil Piston is"; VOLOILP; "m³"
PRINT "Vol Disp of Hyd Cyl Pist Per Int Strok is"; VOLCYL; "m³"
PRINT "Movement of Hydr Cyl Pist Per Int Strok is"; SHYDCYL; "m"
PRINT "Vol Dis of Blk End of Int Air Cyl Pis is"; VOLAIRCY; "m³"
PRINT "Flow Rate of Oil From Intensifier is"; QOILINT; "m³/s"
PRINT "Air Consumpt Rate of Intens is"; QAIRINT; "std m³/min"
END
```

Computer printout answers are as follows:

(a) 2.57×10^{-5} m³ = 0.0257 L   (b) 2.57×10^{-5} m³ = 0.0257 L

(c) 2.26×10^{-2} m = 22.5 mm   (d) 1.64×10^{-3} m³ = 1.64 L

(e) 2.57×10^{-5} m³/s = 0.0257 L/s   (f) 0.709 std m³/min

10-42. Computer Project.

CHAPTER 11   PNEUMATICS - CIRCUITS AND APPLICATIONS

11-1.   1. Safety of operation.
        2. Performance of desired function.
        3. Efficiency of operation.
        4. Costs.

11-2.   Because the air is clean and thus does not contaminate
        the environment.

11-3.   This results in excessive pressure losses due to
        friction.

11-4.   This results in excessive initial installation costs.

11-5.   The compressor must operate at higher output pressure
        which requires greater input power.

11-6.   The compressor must provide a greater flow rate to offset
        the air leaks into the atmosphere.

11-7.   It costs money to provide the input power to drive a
        compressor for providing compressed air at greater than
        atmospheric pressure.

11-8.   Systems where an air vacuum pressure is used to create a
        net force to perform a useful function.

11-9.   1. Materials handling.
        2. Sealing.
        3. Vacuum forming.

11-10. The exact amount of suction pressure developed can not be
        guaranteed.

11-11. Objects to be lifted can not generally weigh more than
        several hundred pounds because the maximum suction
        pressure equals one atmosphere of pressure.

11-12. To reduce the size and power requirements of a pump to
        handle system large transient flow rate conditions.

11-13. 1. Preload after charge gas has been added to ACC.
        2. Charge after pump has been turned on and pressure
           reaches PRV setting.
        3. Final position of ACC piston after load is fully
           driven.

11-14.   First solve for the compression ratio.

$$CR = \frac{125 + 14.7}{14.7} = 9.50$$

From Figure 11 – 2, $d^{5.31} = 1.2892$

Finally, using the Harris Formula, the pressure loss is found.

$$P_f = \frac{0.1025 \, L \, Q^2}{CR \, d^{5.31}} = \frac{0.1025 \times 150 \times \left(\frac{150}{60}\right)^2}{9.50 \times 1.2892} = \underline{7.85 \text{ psi}}$$

11-15.   The total equivalent length of the pipe can be found using Figure 11-3.

$$L = 150 + 3 \times 0.56 + 2 \times 29.4 + 4 \times 1.50 + 5 \times 2.60$$

$$= 150 + 1.68 + 58.8 + 6.0 + 13.0 = 229.5 \text{ ft}$$

Substituting into the Harris Formula yields the answer.

$$P_f = \frac{0.1025 \times 229.5 \times \left(\frac{150}{60}\right)^2}{9.50 \times 1.2892} = \underline{12.0 \text{ psi}}$$

11-16.   First solve for the compression ratio where 1000 kPa gage

$$= 1000 \text{ kPa gage} \times \frac{14.7 \text{ psi}}{101 \text{ kPa}} = 145.5 \text{ psig}$$

$$\text{Compression ratio} = CR = \frac{145.5 + 14.7}{14.7} = 10.9$$

The pipe inside dia. is $d = 25 \text{ mm} \times \frac{1 \text{ in}}{25.4 \text{ mm}} = 0.984 \text{ in}$

Thus $d^{5.31} = 0.984^{5.31} = 0.918$

Finally using the Harris Formula, the pressure loss is found where

$$Q = 3 \frac{m^3}{min} \times \left(\frac{3.28 \text{ ft}}{1 \text{ m}} \right)^3 = 105.9 \text{ scfm} \quad \text{and} \quad L = 100 \text{ m} = 328 \text{ ft}$$

$$P_f = \frac{0.1025 \times 328 \times \left(\frac{105.9}{60} \right)^2}{10.9 \times 0.918} = 10.5 \text{ psi} = 10.5 \text{ psi} \times \frac{101 \text{ kPa}}{14.7 \text{ psi}}$$

$$= \underline{72.1 \text{ kPa}}$$

11-17.   The total equivalent length of the pipe can be found using Figure 11-3 for a 1 inch nominal pipe size.

$$L = 328 + 2 \times 0.56 + 3 \times 29.4 + 5 \times 1.50 + 4 \times 2.60 + 6 \times 1.23$$

$$= 328 + 1.12 + 88.2 + 7.5 + 10.4 + 7.38 = 442.6 \text{ ft}$$

Substituting into the Harris Formula yields the answer.

$$P_f = \frac{0.1025 \times 442.6 \times \left(\frac{105.9}{60} \right)^2}{10.9 \times 0.918} = 14.2 \text{ psi} = \underline{97.6 \text{ kPa}}$$

11-18.   Actual HP to drive compressor $= \dfrac{P_{in}Q}{65.4 \ \eta_o} \left[\left(\dfrac{P_{out}}{P_{in}} \right)^{0.286} - 1 \right]$

$$= \frac{14.7 \times 200}{65.4 \times 0.70} \left[\left(\frac{114.7}{14.7} \right)^{0.286} - 1 \right] = 51.4 \text{ HP} = 38.3 \text{ kW}$$

Electric power required to drive electric motor

$$= \frac{38.3 \text{ kW}}{0.90} = 42.6 \text{ kW}$$

$$\text{Yearly cos t} = 42.6 \text{ kW} \times 4000 \frac{hr}{yr} \times \frac{\$0.10}{kW \ hr} = \underline{\$17,040/yr}$$

11-19.   Actual HP to drive compressor

$$= \frac{14.7 \times 250}{65.4 \times 0.70} \left[\left(\frac{126.7}{14.7} \right)^{0.286} - 1 \right] = 80.3 \text{ HP} = 59.9 \text{ kW}$$

Electric power required to drive electric motor

$$= \frac{59.9 \text{ kW}}{0.90} = 66.6 \text{ kW}$$

$$\text{Yearly cos t} = 66.6 \text{ kW} \times 4000 \frac{\text{hr}}{\text{yr}} \times \frac{\$0.10}{\text{kW hr}} = \$26,640\Big/\text{yr}$$

$$\text{Additional yearly cos t} = \$26,640 - \$17,040 = \underline{\$9,600\Big/\text{yr}}$$

11-20. Actual kW to drive compressor $= \dfrac{P_{in}Q}{17.1 \, \eta_o}\left[\left(\dfrac{P_{out}}{P_{in}}\right)^{0.286} - 1\right]$

$$= \frac{101 \times 6}{17.1 \times 0.70}\left[\left(\frac{791}{101}\right)^{0.286} - 1\right] = 40.6 \text{ kW}$$

Electric power required to drive electric motor

$$= 40.6 \text{ kW}/0.90 = 45.1 \text{ kW}$$

$$\text{Yearly cos t} = 45.1 \text{ kW} \times 4000 \frac{\text{hr}}{\text{yr}} \times \frac{\$0.10}{\text{kW hr}} = \underline{\$18,040\Big/\text{yr}}$$

11-21. Actual kW to drive compressor $= \dfrac{101 \times 7.5}{17.1 \times 0.70}\left[\left(\dfrac{891}{101}\right)^{0.286} - 1\right]$

$$= 54.7 \text{ kW}$$

Electric power required to drive electric motor

$$= 54.7 \text{ kW}/0.9 = 60.8 \text{ kW}$$

$$\text{Yearly cos t} = 60.8 \text{ kW} \times 4000 \frac{\text{hr}}{\text{yr}} \times \frac{\$0.10}{\text{kW hr}} = \$24,320/\text{yr}$$

Additional yearly cost $= \$24,320 - \$18,040 = \underline{\$6,280/\text{yr}}$

11-22. Cylinder extends and retracts continuously.

11-23.   (a) Nothing if fully extended. Extends and stops if fully
             retracted.
         (b) Cylinder extends and retracts continuously when V4
             and V5 are both depressed.

11-24.   (a) Cylinder 1 extends and then cylinder 2 extends.
         (b) Cylinder 2 retracts and then cylinder 1 retracts.

11-25.   Insert a pilot check valve in the line connected to the
         blank end of cylinder 1. The pilot line of the check
         valve should be connected to the line connected to the
         rod end of cylinder 1.

         The direction of the pilot check valve should be such
         that free flow is always allowed into the blank end of
         the cylinder through the pilot check valve even though
         no pilot pressure exists. Reverse flow from the blank
         end of the cylinder requires pilot pressure to be
         exerted on the pilot check valve.

11-26.   1. Actuate V1 only: cylinder moves to the right.
         2. Actuate V2 only: cylinder moves to the left.
         3. Actuate both V1 and V2: cylinder is pneumatically
            locked since both ends are exposed to system air
            pressure.
         4. Unactuate both V1 and V2: cylinder is free to move
            since both ends are vented to the atmosphere.

11-27.   System redesign is shown below:

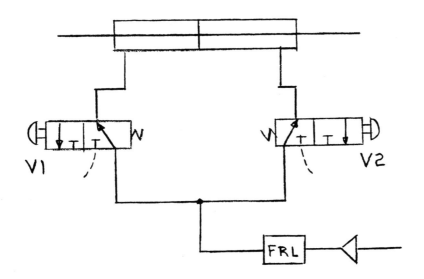

11-28. Cylinder 2 extends through full stroke while cylinder 1 does not move. Then cylinder 1 extends through full stroke.

By adding a properly adjusted flow control valve in each line leading to the blank end of each cylinder, the cylinders will extend and retract together at the same speeds.

11-29. (a) $P_{suction}(abs) = P_{suction}(gage) + P_{atm} = -8 + 14.7 = 6.7 \text{ psia}$

Using Equation 11-4 we have:

$$F = P_{atm}A_o - P_{suction}A_i$$

$$= 14.7 \times \frac{\pi}{4} \times 7^2 - 6.7 \times \frac{\pi}{4} \times 6^2 = 566 - 189 = 377 \text{ lb}$$

Using a factor of safety of 3, we have:

$$W = F/3 = 377/3 = \underline{126 \text{ lb}}$$

(b) $F = P_{atm}A_o = 566 \text{ lb}$ so $W = \frac{566}{3} = \underline{189 \text{ lb}}$

11-30. $t = \frac{V}{Q} \ln\left(\frac{P_{atm}}{P_{vacuum}}\right) = \frac{5}{3} \ln\left(\frac{14.7}{5}\right) = \underline{1.80 \text{ min}}$

11-31. (a) $P_{suction}(abs) = P_{suction}(gage) + P_{atm}$

$$= -50 \text{ kPa} + 101 \text{ kPa} = 51 \text{ kPa abs}$$

Using Equation 11-4, we have:

$$F = P_{atm}A_o - P_{suction}A_i$$

$$= 101,000 \times \frac{\pi}{4} \times 0.100^2 - 51,000 \times \frac{\pi}{4} \times 0.080^2$$

$$= 793 - 256 = 537 \text{ N}$$

Using a factor of safety of 3, we have:

$$W = F/3 = 537/3 = \underline{179 \text{ N}}$$

(b) $F = P_{atm}A_o = 793 \text{ lb}$ so $W = \frac{793}{3} = \underline{264 \text{ N}}$

11-32. $F = W = P_{atm}A_o - P_{suction}A_i$

Since the factor of safety equals 2, we have:

$W_{total} = 2 \times 1500 = 3000$ N $= 6W$

Substituting values into the above equation yields :

$$\frac{3000}{6} = 101{,}000 \times \frac{\pi}{4} \times 0.1^2 - P_{suction} \times \frac{\pi}{4} \times 0.08^2$$

$500 = 793 - 0.00503\, P_{suction}$ or $P_{suction} = 58{,}300$ Pa abs

Also $t = \dfrac{V}{Q} \ln\left(\dfrac{P_{atm}}{P_{suction}}\right)$

Thus $2 = \dfrac{0.20}{Q} \ln\left(\dfrac{101{,}000}{58{,}300}\right)$ so $Q = \underline{0.0550\ \text{std}\ \text{m}^3/\text{min}}$

11-33. Use Equation 10-3 where V_1 = required accumulator size.

$P_1 V_1 = P_2 V_2 = P_3 V_3$ Also we have:

$V_{hydr\ cyl} = V_3 - V_2 = 450\,\text{in}^3$ per statement of problem.

Thus $V_3 = \dfrac{P_2 V_2}{P_3} = \dfrac{3000\, V_2}{1800} = 1.67\, V_2$

Solving the preceding equations yields:

$1.67\, V_2 - V_2 = 450\,\text{in}^3$ or $V_2 = 672\,\text{in}^3$, Thus $V_3 = 1122\,\text{in}^3$

Therefore, we have a solution as follows:

$V_1 = \dfrac{P_2 V_2}{P_1} = \dfrac{3000 \times 672}{1200} = 1680\,\text{in}^3 = \underline{7.27\ \text{gal accumulator}}$

11-34. $F_{load} = P_3 A_{hydr\ cyl} = 1800 \times \dfrac{\pi}{4} \times 6^2 = 50{,}894$ lb

$V_{hydr\ cyl} = \dfrac{\pi}{4} \times 6^2 \times \text{stroke} = 450\,\text{in}^3$,   Thus stroke $= \underline{15.9\ \text{in.}}$

11-35. $P_1 V_1 = P_2 V_2 = P_3 V_3$ where $V_{hydr\ cyl} = V_3 - V_2 = 7370\ cm^3$

$$V_3 = \frac{P_2 V_2}{P_3} = \frac{310\ V_2}{126} = 1.67\ V_2 \qquad \text{Thus we have:}$$

$$1.67\ V_2 - V_2 = 7370 \quad \text{or} \quad V_2 = 11{,}000\ cm^3 \quad \text{and} \quad V_3 = 18{,}370\ cm^3$$

$$\text{So } V_1 = \frac{P_2 V_2}{P_1} = \frac{210 \times 11{,}000}{84} = 27{,}500\ cm^3 = 0.0275\ m^3 = 27.5\ L$$

11-36. $F_{load} = P_3 A_{hydr\ cyl} = \left(126 \times 10^5\right) \times \dfrac{\pi}{4} \times 0.152^2 = 229{,}000\ N$

$$V_{hydr\ cyl} = \frac{\pi}{4} \times 0.152^2 \times \text{stroke} = 0.00737\ m^3$$

Therefore the stroke $= 0.406\ m = \underline{406\ mm}$

11-37. $\dfrac{P_1 V_1}{T_1} = \dfrac{P_2 V_2}{T_2}$ Thus we have:

$$P_2 = \frac{T_2}{T_1} \times \frac{V_1}{V_2} \times P_1 = \frac{180 + 273}{40 + 273} \times \frac{0.04}{0.03} \times 10\ MPa = \underline{19.3\ MPa}$$

11-38. $\dfrac{P_1 V_1}{T_1} = \dfrac{P_2 V_2}{T_2}$ Thus we have:

$$P_1 = \frac{T_1}{T_2} \times \frac{V_2}{V_1} \times P_2 = \frac{200 + 460}{100 + 460} \times \frac{275}{180} \times 1000\ psi = \underline{1800\ psi}$$

11-39. The computer program is written as follows:


```
PRINT "Computer Analysis of the Compressor of Exercise 11-18"
INPUT "Enter the Compressor Input Pressure(psig):", PIN
INPUT "Enter the Compressor Efficiency(%):", COMPEFF
INPUT "Enter the Compressor Output Pressure(psig):", POUT
INPUT "Enter the Electric Motor Efficiency(%):", MOTEFF
INPUT "Enter the Compressor Flowrate(SCFM):", Q
INPUT "Enter the Cost of Electricity($/kW hr):", COSTKWHR
INPUT "Enter the Number of Hours Per Year(hr/yr):", N
```

```
R = (POUT + 14.7) / (PIN + 14.7)
REXP = R ^ .286
REXP1 = REXP - 1
ACTHP = (PIN + 14.7) * Q * REXP1 / (65.4 * COMPEFF * .01)
ACTKW = ACTHP * .746
ELECPRW = ACTKW / (MOTEFF * .01)
YRCOST = ELECPRW * N * COSTKWHR

PRINT "Yearly Cost of Electricity is"; YRCOST; "$/yr"
END
```

The following are the results of executing the computer program for the five different values of output pressure:

Output Pressure (psig)	Yearly Cost of Electricity ($/yr)
80	14,983
90	16,039
100	17,026
110	17,953
120	18,829

11-40.   Computer Project.

CHAPTER 12   FLUID LOGIC CONTROL SYSTEMS

12-1.   Fluidics is the technology that utilizes fluid flow
          phenomenon in components and circuits to perform a wide
          variety of control functions. These include sensing,
          logic, memory, timing and interfacing to other control
          media.

12-2.   1. Unique sensing capabilities.
          2. Remarkable maintainability.
          3. Environmental immunity.
          4. Long-term reliability.

12-3.   Fluidic components operate at low power and pressure
          levels (normally below 15 psi). Yet these low pressure
          fluidic signals can reliably control hydraulic systems
          operating with up to 10,000 psi oil to provide the
          muscle to do useful work at rates up to several hundred
          horsepower.

12-4.   An AND function is one which requires that two or more
          control signals exist in order to obtain an output.

12-5.   An OR function is one in which all control signals must
          be off in order for the output to not exist. Therefore,
          any one control signal will produce an output.

12-6.   Drawings A and B in Figure 12-15 illustrate the Coanda
          Effect phenomenon. As shown in Drawing A, a jet of air
          (from the supply port) is emitted into a confined region
          at a velocity high enough to produce turbulent flow.
          This turbulent jet behaves very much like a jet pump and
          entrains air from its surroundings. As a result, a flow
          is established along the walls of the confined region.
          This air flow rushes in to replace the air being pumped
          out by the power jet.

          Since a turbulent jet is dynamically unstable, it will
          veer rapidly back and forth. When the jet veers close to
          one wall, it interrupts the flow path along the wall on
          that side as shown in Drawing B. The result is that no
          more air is flowing on that side to replace the air
          being pumped out by the power jet. This constricted flow
          causes a lowering of pressure on that side of the power
          nozzle. This generates a low pressure bubble next to the
          jet. The low pressure bubble causes the stream to become
          stable and remain attached to that wall.

12-7.   A flip-flop is a bistable digital control device. Thus, a flip-flop has two stable states when all control signals are OFF. However, each of the two stable states is predictable as shown by the truth table in Figure 12-18. For the operation of a flip-flop, refer to Figure 12-17.

12-8.   A bistable device has two stable states whereas a monostable device has only one stable state.

12-9.   In some applications it is necessary to have a specific output when the power supply is first turned ON and all control signals are OFF. For these applications, a flip-flop with a start-up preference is used. Figure 12-19 shows such a flip-flow with its symbol (note + sign) and truth table. As shown, when all control signals are OFF, the output is ON at 02 and OFF at 01. Otherwise it behaves exactly the same as does a basic flip-flop.

12-10.   A SRT flip-flop has the same capabilities as a basic flip-flop except it can switch by applying a signal to the trigger port. S and R stand for SET and RESET respectively and perform as regular control signals. T stands for trigger and whenever it is applied, it complements (switches) the output. Figure 12-20 shows the symbol and truth table for a SRT flip-flop.

12-11.   An OR gate is a device which will have an output if any one or any combination of control signals is ON. An exclusive OR gate is a device which will have an output only if one control signal (but not any combination of control signals) is ON.

12-12.   The back-pressure sensor works on the principle that the pressure drop across a nozzle or orifice increases with flow through that nozzle (See Figure 12-25 for operation). A proximity sensor is a device which emits a high velocity jet of supply air. When an object comes near, a portion of the supply jet is reflected from the object. This increases the pressure at the output port to permit the switching of an appropriate component as shown in Figure 12-27b. A proximity sensor permits the detection of objects at greater distances than is possible with back-pressure devices.

12-13.   The interruptible jet sensor uses a nozzle to transmit an air stream across a gap to a receiver. When the flow is unobstructed, adequate pressure is recovered by the

144

receiver to hold the fluidic element in a particular mode (See Figure 12-28a). However, when an object enters the jet area, the output pressure in the receiver is reduced to cause the fluidic element to switch to the opposite mode (See Figure 12-28b).

12-14. An OR/NOR KEY is a back-pressure sensor.

12-15. Contact sensing is accomplished by the sensing of objects by physical contact. It is usually done by a moving-part device called a limit valve or limit switch (See Figure 12-29).

12-16. A clean air supply is an absolute necessity for trouble-free operation of fluidic systems. Contaminants can obstruct critical passageways of fluidic components.

12-17. Moving part logic devices are miniature valve-type devices which by the action of internal moving parts, perform switching operations in fluid logic systems.

12-18. 1. Mechanical displacement.
2. Electric voltage.
3. Fluid pressure.

12-19. Fluidic devices have no moving parts.

12-20. Moving part logic devices do not have critical flow passageways which can clog due to contaminants in the air.

12-21. Since fluidic devices have no moving parts, they virtually do not wear out.

12-22. Strict maintenance procedures for providing a clean supply of air and unobstructed component passageways must be established and rigidly followed.

12-23. 1. It provides a means by which a logic circuit can be reduced to its simplest form.
2. It allows for the quick synthesis of a circuit which is to perform desired logic operations.

12-24. Multiplication and addition are permitted.

12-25. Logic inversion is the process that makes the output signal not equal to the input signal in terms of ON versus OFF.

12-26. The commutative law states that the order in which
        variables appear in equations is irrelevant.

        An example is: A + B = B + A

        The associative law states that the order in which
        functions are performed is irrelevant, provided that the
        functions are unchanged. An example is as follows:

        A + B + C = (A + B) + C = A + (B + C) = (A + C) + B

12-27. DeMorgan's Theorem allows for the inversion of functions
        as follows:

        (I) $\overline{A + B + C} = \overline{A} \bullet \overline{B} \bullet \overline{C}$

        The inversion of the function (A or B or C) equals the
        function (not A and not B and not C).

        (II) $\overline{A \bullet B \bullet C} = \overline{A} + \overline{B} + \overline{C}$

        The inversion of the function (A and B and C) equals
        the function (not A or not B or not C).

12-28. (a) Switch the outputs of the flip-flop to the opposite
            sides of the Interface Valve. Also move the
            interruptible jets as close as possible to the ends
            of the hydraulic cylinder.

        (b) When the present system with a preferenced flip-flop
            is initially started, the cylinder rod will always
            begin by moving to the right. If the preferenced flip-
            flop is replaced by a regular flip-flop, the system
            may start up with the cylinder beginning its move to
            the left or to the right. The starting direction is
            indeterminant.

12-29.

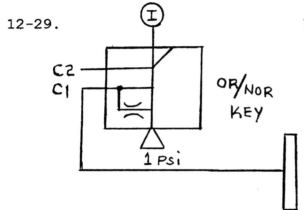

When door is open, air pressure
turns indicator ON.

Door 1 or 2 in closed position
(C1 is blocked).

146

12-30. (a) The cylinder extends, retracts and stops. Thus, we have one cycle of reciprocation.

(b) The cylinder extends and retracts continuously. Thus, we have continuous reciprocation.

12-31. (a) Nothing.

(b) The cylinder extends, retracts and stops. Thus, we have one cycle of reciprocation.

12-32. No. At the completion of the extension stroke, the cylinder will automatically reverse even though one or both buttons are still held. It retracts fully and another cycle cannot be started until both buttons are released and re-actuated. This is because the cylinder cannot extend until all three control signals have been removed from the OR gate which receives one of its three control signals from the output of the flip-flop.

The bottom control signal to this OR gate is removed on the previous cycle when both buttons are released. The two top signals to this OR gate are removed when both buttons are pressed to start the next cycle.

12-33. Both cylinders extend together. Then both cylinders retract together. End of cycle.

12-34. 2 variables produce $2^2 = 4$ possible combinations.

A	B	A + B	A • (A + B)
0	0	0	0
1	0	1	1
0	1	1	0
1	1	1	1

12-35. 3 variables produce $2^3 = 8$ possible combinations.

A	B	C	A + B	B + C	(A + B) + C	A + (B + C)
0	0	0	0	0	0	0
1	0	0	1	0	1	1
1	1	0	1	1	1	1
1	0	1	1	1	1	1
0	1	0	1	1	1	1
0	0	1	0	1	1	1
0	1	1	1	1	1	1
1	1	1	1	1	1	1

12-36.

A	B	A $\bullet$ B	$\overline{A \bullet B}$	$\overline{A}$	$\overline{B}$	$\overline{A} + \overline{B}$
0	0	0	1	1	1	1
1	0	0	1	0	1	1
0	1	0	1	1	0	1
1	1	1	0	0	0	0

12-37.

A	B	C	B + C	A $\bullet$ (B + C)	A $\bullet$ B	A $\bullet$ C	(A $\bullet$ B) + (A $\bullet$ C)
0	0	0	0	0	0	0	0
1	0	0	0	0	0	0	0
1	1	0	1	1	1	0	1
1	0	1	1	1	0	1	1
0	1	0	1	0	0	0	0
0	0	1	1	0	0	0	0
0	1	1	1	0	0	0	0
1	1	1	1	1	1	1	1

12-38.

A	B	$\overline{A}$	$\overline{A}$ + B	A $\bullet$ ($\overline{A}$ + B)	A $\bullet$ B
0	0	1	1	0	0
0	1	1	1	0	0
1	0	0	0	0	0
1	1	0	1	1	1

12-39. From DeMorgan's Theorem we have:

$$\overline{A \bullet B \bullet C} = \overline{A} + \overline{B} + \overline{C}$$

Hence $A \bullet B \bullet C = \overline{\overline{(A \bullet B \bullet C)}} = \overline{(\overline{A} + \overline{B} + \overline{C})} = \text{NOT} (\overline{A} + \overline{B} + \overline{C})$

Therefore to generate the AND function, we invert individual inputs and connect the inverted inputs to a NOR gate. The NOR gates are used to invert the input signals as shown below.

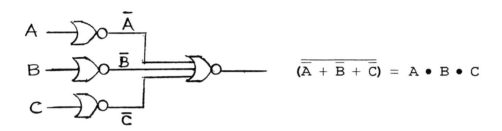

$$\overline{(\overline{A} + \overline{B} + \overline{C})} = A \bullet B \bullet C$$

12-40. From DeMorgan's Theorem we have:

$$Z = \overline{A} + \overline{B} + \overline{C} = \overline{(A \bullet B \bullet C)}$$

This means we need to generate the NAND function of inputs A, B and C as shown below.

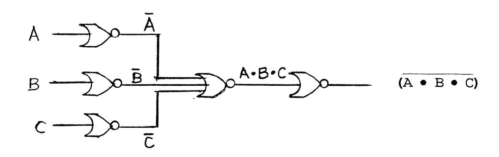

$$\overline{(A \bullet B \bullet C)}$$

149

12-41.　When the cylinder is fully retracted, the signals from A1 and A2 are both ON. The extension stroke begins when push button P is pressed since the output P • A1 of the AND gate produces an output Q from the Flip Flop. The push button can be released because the Flip Flop maintains its Q output even though P • A1 is OFF.

When the cylinder is fully extended, A2 is OFF, causing $\overline{A2}$ to go ON switching the Flip Flop to output $\overline{Q}$. This removes the signal to the DCV which retracts the cylinder. The push button must be again pressed to produce another cycle. If the push button is held depressed, the cycle repeats continuously.

12-42.　When the guard is open (M is OFF and $\overline{M}$ is ON), the output of the Flip Flop is Q. Closing the guard turns M ON and produces an output to the DCV from the AND gate. This causes the cylinder to extend. When the cylinder is fully extended, signal A goes OFF, signal $\overline{A}$ goes ON, and the Flip Flop output shifts to $\overline{Q}$. This shifts the DCV which retracts the cylinder.

At the end of the cylinder retraction stroke, Flip Flop inputs S and R are both OFF, and Q remains OFF. Thus the cylinder remains fully retracted. When the guard is opened again (M is OFF), the Flip Flop switches to the Q output to prepare the system for the next cycle.

12-43.　$P = A \bullet (A + B) = A \bullet A + A \bullet B$

$P = A + A \bullet B$ 　(using Theorem 6)

Thus output P is ON when A is ON, or A and B are ON. Therefore control Signal B (applied to valve 3) is not needed.

CHAPTER 13   ELECTRICAL CONTROLS FOR FLUID POWER CIRCUITS

13-1.   One of the reasons for this trend is that more machines are being designed for automatic operation to be controlled with electrical signals from computers.

13-2.   Pressure switches open or close their contacts based on system pressure. A temperature switch opens or closes an electrical switch when a predetermined temperature is reached.

13-3.   Limit switches open and close circuits when they are actuated at the end of the retraction or extension strokes of hydraulic or pneumatic cylinders. Push button switches are actuated manually.

13-4.   A relay is an electrically actuated switch. As shown in Figure 13-8(a), when switch 1-SW is closed, the coil is energized. This pulls on the spring-loaded relay arm to open the upper set of normally closed contacts and close the lower set of normally open contacts. Figure 13-8(b) shows the symbol for the relay coil and the symbols for the normally open and closed contacts.

13-5.   Timers are used in electrical control circuits when a time delay is required from the instant of actuation to the closing of contacts.

13-6.   Electrical switches possess virtually no resistance.

13-7.   An indicator lamp is often used to indicate the state of a specific circuit component. For example, indicator lamps are used to determine which solenoid operator of a directional control valve is energized.

13-8.   1. Higher pressures increase internal leakage inside pumps, actuators and valves.

   2. Temperature changes affect fluid viscosity and thus, leakage.

13-9.   1. Velocity Transducer: senses the linear or angular velocity of the system output and generates a signal proportional to the measured velocity.

2. _Positional Transducer_: senses the linear or angular position of the system output and generates a signal proportional to the measured position.

13-10. A feedback transducer is a device which performs the function of converting one source of energy into another such as mechanical to electrical.

13-11. A servo valve replaces the flow control valve and directional control valve of an open-loop system.

13-12. The transfer function of a component or a total system is defined as the output divided by the input.

13-13. Deadband is that region or band of no response where an input signal will not cause an output. Hysteresis is the difference between the response of a component to an increasing signal and the response to a decreasing signal.

13-14. Open loop gain is the gain (output divided by input) from the error signal to the feedback signal.

13-15. Closed loop transfer function is the system output divided by the system input.

13-16. Repeatable error is the discrepancy between the actual output position and the programmed output position.

13-17. Tracking error is the distance by which the output lags the input command signal while the load is moving.

13-18. The forward path contains the amplifier, servo valve and cylinder. The feedback path contains the transducer.

13-19. A programmable logic controller (PLC) is a user-friendly electronic computer designed to perform logic functions such as AND, OR and NOT for controlling the operation of industrial equipment and processes.

13-20. Unlike general purpose computers, a PLC is designed to operate in industrial environments where high ambient temperature and humidity levels may exist.

13-21. A PLC consists of solid—state digital logic elements (rather than electromechanical relays) for making logic decisions and providing corresponding outputs.

13-22. 1. Electromechanical relays have to be hard-wired to
           perform specific functions.
        2. PLCs are more reliable and faster in operation.
        3. PLCs are smaller in size and can be more readily
           expanded.

13-23. (a) CPU: receives input data from various sensing devices
            such as switches, executes the stored program, and
            delivers corresponding output signals to various load
            control devices such as relay coils and solenoids.

        (b) Programmer/Monitor: allows the user to enter the
            desired program into the RAM memory of the CPU as
            well as edit, monitor, and run the program.

        (c) I/O Module: transforms the various signals received
            from or sent to the fluid power interface devices
            such as push button switches, pressure switches,
            limit switches, motor relay coils, solenoid coils and
            indicator lights.

13-24. ROM memory cannot be changed during operation or lost
        when electrical power to the CPU is turned off. RAM
        memory which is lost when electrical power is removed,
        can be programmed and altered by the user.

13-25. The cylinder extends, retracts and stops.

13-26. Cylinder 1 extends.
        Cylinder 2 extends.
        Both cylinders remain extended until 1-SW is opened.
        Then both cylinders retract together and stop.

13-27. (a) Cylinder 1 extends.
            Cylinder 2 extends.

        (b) Cylinders 1 and 2 retract together.

13-28. When push button switch 1-PB is actuated, coil 1-CR is
        energized. This closes normally open contacts 1-CR which
        energizes SOL A and holds. Thus, the cylinder extends
        until limit switch 1-LS is actuated. This opens the
        contacts of 1-LS which de-energizes coil 1-CR. As a
        result, the contacts for 1-CR are returned back to their
        normally open mode and SOL A is de-energized. This
        shifts the DCV back into its spring offset mode to
        retract the cylinder.

If push button 2-PB is actuated while the cylinder is extending, the cylinder will immediately stop and then retract. This is because coil 1-CR is de-energized which returns the contacts for 1-CR back to their normally open mode. This de-energizes SOL A which shifts the DCV into its spring offset mode.

13-29. (a) Cylinder 1 extends.
        Cylinder 2 extends.
        Cylinders 1 and 2 start to retract together but as soon as limit switch 1-LS is actuated, SOL B and D are de-energized. Thus, both DCVs go into their spring-centered mode and both cylinders stop.

        (b) If 2-PB is depressed momentarily while cylinder 1 is extending, cylinder 1 stops and nothing else happens. If 2-PB is depressed momentarily while cylinder 2 is extending, the system behaves the same as described in part (a) above. Thus, there is no effect on the operation of the system.

13-30. $\omega_H = A \sqrt{\dfrac{2\beta}{VM}} = 4\sqrt{\dfrac{2 \times 200,000}{40 \times \dfrac{750}{386}}} = 287 \,\, \text{rad}/\text{s}$

Open loop gain $= \dfrac{\omega_H}{3} = \dfrac{95.7}{\text{s}}$

$G_{sv} = \dfrac{\text{open loop gain}}{G_A \times G_{cyl} \times H} = \dfrac{95.7}{G_A \times 0.15 \times 3.5} = \dfrac{182}{G_A}$

$RE = \dfrac{\text{system deadband}}{G_A \times H} = \dfrac{3.5}{G_A \times 3.5} = 0.002$

Hence $G_A = 500 \,\, \text{ma}/\text{v}$ and $G_{sv} = \underline{0.364 \left(\text{in}^3/\text{s}\right)/\text{ma}}$

13-31. Closed loop transfer function $= \dfrac{G}{1 + GH}$

$G = G_A G_{sv} G_{cyl} = 55 \times 0.364 \times 0.15 = 27.3 \,\, \text{in}/\text{v}$

Closed loop transfer function $= \dfrac{27.3}{1 + 27.3 \times 3.5} = \underline{0.283 \,\, \text{in}/\text{v}}$

13-32. $\omega_H = A\sqrt{\dfrac{2\beta}{VM}} = 25 \times 10^{-4}\sqrt{\dfrac{2 \times (1400 \times 10^6)}{(750 \times 10^{-6}) \times 300}} = 279 \ \dfrac{rad}{s}$

Open loop gain $= \dfrac{\omega_H}{3} = \dfrac{93}{s}$

$G_{SV} = \dfrac{\text{open loop gain}}{G_A \times G_{CYL} \times H} = \dfrac{93}{G_A \times 0.04 \times 1.75} = \dfrac{1330}{G_A}$

$RE = \dfrac{\text{system deadband}}{G_A \times H} = \dfrac{3.5}{G_A \times 1.75} = 0.004$

Hence $G_A = 500 \ \dfrac{ma}{V}$ and $G_{SV} = 2.66 \ \left(\dfrac{cm^3}{s}\right) / ma$

13-33. Closed loop transfer function $= \dfrac{G}{1 + GH}$

$G = G_A G_{SV} G_{CYL} = 500 \times 2.66 \times 0.04 = 53.2 \ \dfrac{cm}{V}$

Closed loop transfer function $= \dfrac{53.2}{1 + 53.2 \times 1.75} = 0.565 \ \dfrac{cm}{V}$

13-34. $TE = \dfrac{\text{S. V. max. current (ma)}}{G_A\left(\dfrac{ma}{V}\right) \times H\left(\dfrac{V}{in}\right)} = \dfrac{250}{55 \times 3.5} = 0.143 \ \text{inches}$

13-35. $TE = \dfrac{\text{S. V. max. current (ma)}}{G_A\left(\dfrac{ma}{V}\right) \times H\left(\dfrac{V}{cm}\right)} = \dfrac{250}{500 \times 1.75} = 0.286 \ cm$

13-36.

C = A • B B is energized when A and B are actuated.

E = A • D E is energized when A and D are actuated.

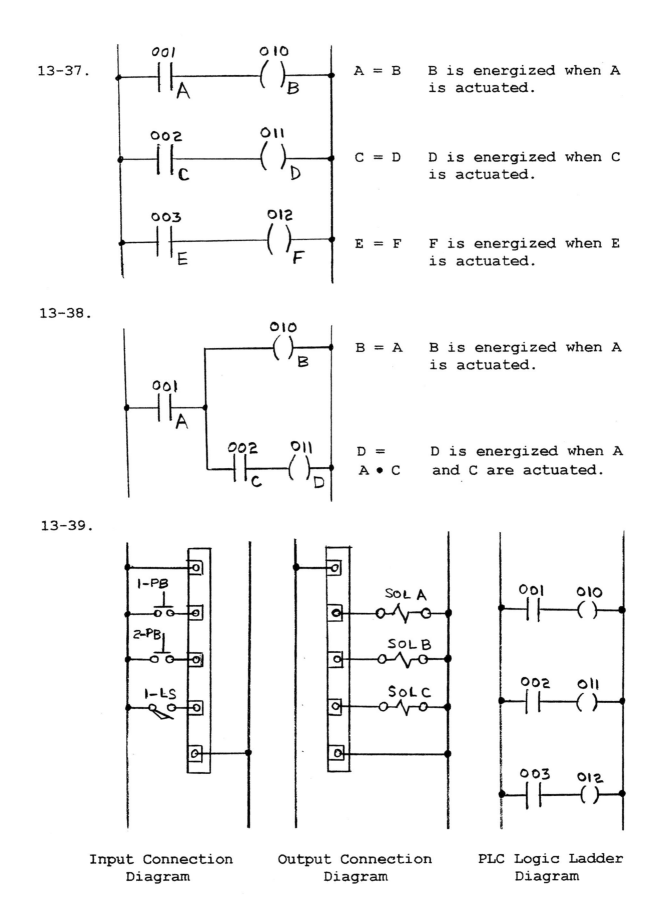

13-37.

A = B   B is energized when A is actuated.

C = D   D is energized when C is actuated.

E = F   F is energized when E is actuated.

13-38.

B = A   B is energized when A is actuated.

D = A • C   D is energized when A and C are actuated.

13-39.

Input Connection Diagram   Output Connection Diagram   PLC Logic Ladder Diagram

156

13-40. Electrical relays are not included in the I/O connection diagram since their functions are replaced by internal control relays.

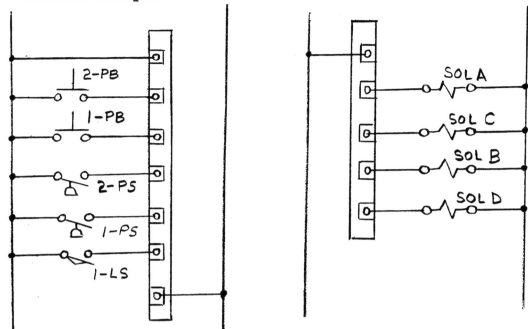

Input Connection Diagram   Output Connection Diagram

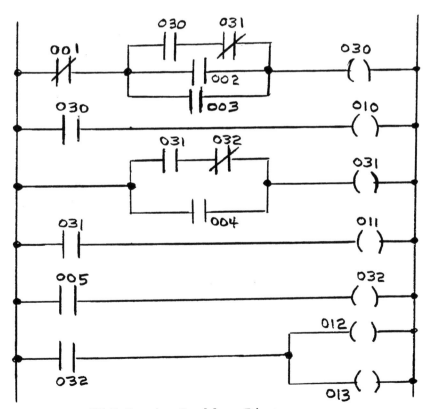

PLC Logic Ladder Diagram

157

13-41.

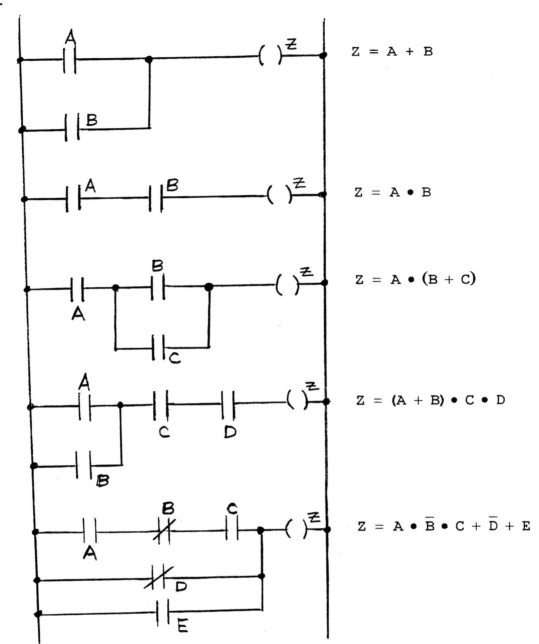

$Z = A + B$

$Z = A \bullet B$

$Z = A \bullet (B + C)$

$Z = (A + B) \bullet C \bullet D$

$Z = A \bullet \bar{B} \bullet C + \bar{D} + E$

CHAPTER 14   FLUID POWER MAINTENANCE AND SAFETY

14-1.   1. Clogged or dirty oil filters.
         2. Inadequate supply of oil in the reservoir.
         3. Leaking seals.
         4. Loose inlet lines which cause the pump to take in
            air.

14-2.   Over half of all hydraulic system problems have been
         traced directly to the oil.

14-3.   1. The type of symptoms encountered, how they were
            detected, and the date.
         2. A description of the maintenance repairs performed.
            This should include the replacement of parts, the
            amount of downtime and the date.

14-4.   Positive seals do not allow any leakage whatsoever
         (external or internal). Non-positive seals (such as the
         clearance used to provide a lubricating film between a
         valve spool and its housing bore) permit a small amount
         of internal leakage.

14-5.   Internal leak: leakage past piston rings in hydraulic
         cylinders.
         External leak: leakage through pipe fittings which have
         become loose.

14-6.   Static seals are used between mating parts which do not
         move relative to each other. Dynamic seals are assembled
         between mating parts which do move relative to each
         other.

14-7.   At very high pressures, O-rings may extrude into the
         clearance space between mating parts as shown in Figure
         14-6. This extrusion is prevented by installing a back-
         up ring as illustrated in Figure 14-6.

14-8.   1. V-ring packings.
         2. Piston cup packings.
         3. Piston rings.

14-9.   Wiper seals are not designed to seal against pressure.
         Instead they are designed to prevent foreign abrasive or
         corrosive materials from entering a cylinder. As such,
         they provide insurance against rod scoring and add
         materially to packing life.

14-10. 1. Leather
        2. Buna-N
        3. Silicone
        4. Neopreme

14-11. A durometer (See Figure 14-15) is an instrument used to
        measure the indentation hardness of rubber and rubber-
        like materials.

14-12. 1. It must make allowance for dirt and chips to settle
           and for air to escape.
        2. It must be able to hold all the oil that might drain
           into the reservoir from the system.
        3. It must maintain the oil level high enough to prevent
           a "whirlpool" effect at the pump inlet line opening.
           Otherwise air will be drawn into the pump.
        4. It should have a surface area large enough to
           dissipate most of the heat generated by the system.

14-13. A filter is a device whose primary function is to retain,
        by some porous medium, insoluble contaminants from a
        fluid. Basically, a strainer is a coarse filter.
        Strainers are constructed of a wire screen which rarely
        contains openings less than 0.0059 inches. Thus, a
        strainer removes only the larger particles.

14-14. 1. Built into the system during component maintenance and
           assembly.
        2. Generated within system during operation.
        3. Introduced into system from external environment.

14-15. One micron is 1 millionth of a meter or 0.000039 inches.
        Therefore, ten microns is 0.00039 in. A ten-micron
        filter is one capable of removing contaminants as small
        as ten microns in size.

14-16. 1. Mechanical
        2. Absorbent
        3. Adsorbent

14-17. An indicating filter is one which contains an indicating
        element which signals the operator when cleaning is
        required.

14-18. 1. Proportional flow filter in separate drain line.
        2. Full flow filter in suction line.

3. Full flow filter in pressure line.
4. Full flow filter in return line.

14-19.   The purpose of a heat exchanger is to add heat or remove
         heat from the fluid of a hydraulic system so that the
         fluid temperature does not become too low or too high.

14-20.   1. Flow meters.
         2. Pressure gages.
         3. Temperature gages.

14-21.   When troubleshooting hydraulic circuits, it should be
         kept in mind that a pump produces the flow of a fluid.
         However, there must be resistance to flow in order to
         have pressure.

14-22.   1. Air entering pump inlet.
         2. Misalignment of pump and drive unit.
         3. Excessive oil viscosity.
         4. Dirty inlet strainer.
         5. Chattering relief valve.

14-23.   1. Air in the fluid.
         2. Pressure relief valve set too low.
         3. Pressure relief valve not properly seated.
         4. Leak in hydraulic line.

14-24.   1. Pump turning in wrong direction.
         2. Ruptured hydraulic line.
         3. Low oil level in reservoir.
         4. Pressure relief valve stuck open.

14-25.   1. Faulty pump.
         2. Directional control valve fails to shift.
         3. System pressure too low.
         4. Defective actuator.
         5. Actuator load is excessive.

14-26.   1. Air in system.
         2. Viscosity of fluid too high.
         3. Worn or damaged pump.
         4. Pump speed too low.
         5. Excessive leakage through actuators or valves.

14-27.   1. Heat exchanger turned off or faulty.
         2. Undersized components or piping.
         3. Incorrect fluid.
         4. Continuous operation of pressure relief valve.

5. Overloaded system.
6. Reservoir too small.

14-28. OSHA stands for the Occupational Safety and Health Administration of the Department of Labor. OSHA is attempting to prevent safety hazards which can be harmful to the health and safety of personnel.

14-29. 1. Workplace Standards: In this category are included the safety of floors, entrance and exit areas, sanitation and fire protection.

2. Machines and Equipment Standards: Important items are machine guards, inspection and maintenance techniques, safety devices and the mounting, anchoring and grounding of fluid power equipment. Of big concern are noise levels produced by operating equipment.

3. Materials Standards: These standards cover items such as toxic fumes, explosive dust particles and excessive atmospheric contamination.

4. Employee Standards: Concerns here include employee training, personnel protective equipment and medical and first air services.

5. Power Source Standards: Standards are applied to power sources such as electric, hydraulic, pneumatic and steam supply systems.

6. Process Standards: Many industrial processes are included such as welding, spraying, abrasive blasting, part dipping and machining.

7. Administrative Regulations: Industry has many administrative responsibilities which it must meet. These include the displaying of OSHA posters stating the rights and responsibilities of both the employer and employees. Industry is also required to keep safety records on accidents, illnesses and other exposure-type occurrences. An annual summary must also be posted.

It is important that safety be incorporated into hydraulic systems to insure compliance with OSHA regulations. The basic rule to follow is that there should be no compromise when it comes to the health and safety of people at the place of their employment.

14-30. Pumps do not pump pressure. Instead they produce fluid flow. The resistance to this flow, produced by the hydraulic system, is what determines pressure. Low oil level in the reservoir could be a cause of no pressure even though there is nothing wrong with the pump.

14-31. This is a research project for students who should request literature from reservoir manufacturing firms.

1. Flat top design shown in Figure 14-16.

2. L-shaped design which consists of a vertical tank mounted on one side of a wide base. The other side of the base is used to mount the pump. Since the tank oil level is higher than the pump inlet, the possibility of cavitation is reduced due to the positive pump inlet pressure.

3. Overhead stack design which uses one or more modular frames which can be stacked in a vertical direction. Each frame contains its own pump and all the pumps (when more than one is used) receive oil from the single oil tank located on top. Since the tank oil level is higher than any of the pump inlets, the possibility of cavitation is reduced.

14-32. The purpose of a reservoir breather is to allow the reservoir to breathe as the oil level changes due to system demand requirements. In this way, the tank is always vented to the atmosphere.

14-33. The purpose of the baffle plate is to separate the pump inlet line from the return line to prevent the same fluid from re-circulating continuously within the tank. In this way all the fluid is uniformly used by the system.

14-34. An excessive pressure drop occurs across the filter resulting in reduced pressure downstream of the filter. This can adversely affect the operation of the pump (starved pump resulting in cavitation) and actuators (slow or no motion) depending on filter location. A filter containing a bypass relief valve, assures non-excessive pressure drop and thus adequate flow no matter how dirt-clogged the filter might become. However filtration no longer is accomplished until the filter is replaced.

14-35. Cylinder friction is influenced by the type of materials in sliding contact, the type of fluid lubricating the sliding surfaces, and the magnitude of the normal force between the mating surfaces.

14-36. Heat generation rate, oil flow rate and allowable oil temperature.

14-37. The nominal rating is the micron value specified for which 95% of entering particles of size greater than the nominal rating will be trapped. The absolute rating represents the size of the largest opening or pore in the filter and thus indicates the largest size particle that could pass through the filter.

14-38. The prevention of the hydraulic fluid from providing lubrication of moving internal members of hydraulic components such as pumps, hydraulic motors, valves and actuators.

14-39. Contaminants can collect inside the clearance between moving mating parts and thus block lubricant flow. Also contaminants can rub against mating surfaces causing a breakdown in the fluid lubricating film.

14-40. 1. Free air.
        2. Entrained gas.
        3. Dissolved air.

14-41. Vapor pressure is defined as the pressure at which a liquid starts to boil (vaporize) and thus begin changing into a vapor (gas).

14-42. Cavitation is the formation and collapse of vapor bubbles.

14-43. As the vapor bubbles are exposed to the high pressure at the outlet port of a pump, the bubbles are collapsed thereby creating extremely high local fluid velocities. This high velocity fluid impacts on internal metal surfaces of the pump. The resulting high impact forces, cause flaking or pitting of the surfaces of the internal components such as gear teeth, vanes and pistons. This results in premature pump failure.

14-44. Pump manufacturers specify a minimum allowable vacuum pressure at the pump inlet port based on the type of fluid being pumped, the maximum operating temperature and the rated pump speed.

14-45.   1. Keep suction velocities below 5 ft/s (1.5 m/s).
      2. Keep pump inlet lines as short as possible.
      3. Mount the pump as close as possible to the reservoir.
      4. Minimize the number of fittings in the pump inlet line.
      5. Use low pressure drop pump inlet filters.
      6. Use a properly designed reservoir.
      7. Use the proper oil recommended by the pump manufacturer.
      8. Keep the oil temperature from exceeding the recommended maximum level (usually 150°F/65°C).

14-46. $\text{Reservoir Size (gal)} = 3 \times \text{Pump Flowrate (gpm)}$

$$= 3 \times 15 = \underline{45 \text{ gal}}$$

14-47. $\text{Reservoir Size (m}^3) = 3 \times \text{Pump Flowrate} \left(\frac{m^3}{s}\right)$

$$= 3 \times 0.001 = \underline{0.003 \text{ m}^3}$$

14-48.   First, calculate the horsepower lost and convert to the heat generation rate in units of BTU/min.

$$HP = \frac{P(psi) \times Q(gpm)}{1714} = \frac{2000 \times 15}{1714} = 17.5 \text{ HP}$$

BTU/min = HP x 42.4 = 17.5 x 42.4 = 742 BTU/min

Next, calculate the oil flow rate in units of lb/min.

Oil flow rate(lb/min) = 7.42 x oil flow rate(gpm)

$$= 7.42 \times 15 = 111.3 \text{ lb/min}$$

The temperature increase is found using Equation 14-5.

$$\text{Temperature Increase} = \frac{742}{0.42 \times 111.3} = 15.9° \text{ F}$$

Downstream oil temperature = 130 + 15.9 = $\underline{145.9°F}$

14-49.

$$\text{Power (kW)} = \frac{P(\text{Pa}) \times Q\left(\frac{m^3}{s}\right)}{1000} = \frac{\left(14 \times 10^6\right) \times \left(1000 \times 10^{-6}\right)}{1000} = 10 \text{ kW}$$

Oil flow rate = 895 x 0.001 = 0.895 kg/s

$$\text{Temperature increase} = \frac{14}{1.8 \times 0.895} = 8.7^\circ \text{ C}$$

Downstream oil temperature = 60 + 8.7 = 68.7°C

14-50.
$$\text{Pump HP Loss} = 0.18 \times \frac{2000 \times 15}{1714} = 3.15$$

$$\text{PRV Average HP Loss} = 0.60 \times \frac{2000 \times 15}{1714} = 10.50$$

$$\text{Line Average HP Loss} = (1.00 - 0.60) \times 0.15 \times \frac{2000 \times 15}{1714} = 1.05$$

Total Average HP Loss = 14.70 HP

Heat Exchanger Rating = 14.70 x 2544 = 37,397 BTU/hr

14-51.
$$\text{Pump kW Loss} = 0.18 \times \frac{\left(14 \times 10^6\right) \times \left(1000 \times 10^{-6}\right)}{1000} = 2.52$$

$$\text{PRV Average kW Loss} = 0.60 \times \frac{\left(14 \times 10^6\right) \times \left(1000 \times 10^{-6}\right)}{1000} = 8.40$$

$$\text{Line Average kW Loss} = 0.40 \times 0.15 \times \frac{\left(14 \times 10^6\right) \times \left(1000 \times 10^{-6}\right)}{1000}$$

$$= 0.84$$

Total kW Loss = 11.76 kW

14-52. Specific heat of oil = 0.42 $\frac{\text{BTU}}{\text{lb}} /^\circ \text{F}$ = 1.8 $\frac{\text{kJ}}{\text{kg}} /^\circ \text{C}$

Thus $\quad 0.42 \ \dfrac{\text{BTU}}{\text{lb} \bullet {}^\circ \text{F}} = 1.8 \ \dfrac{\text{kJ}}{\text{kg} \bullet {}^\circ \text{C}}$

Hence $\dfrac{0.42}{0.42}$ BTU $= \dfrac{1.8}{0.42} \dfrac{\text{kJ}}{\text{kg} \bullet {}^{\circ}\text{C}} \times \dfrac{2.20 \text{ lb}}{2.20} \times \dfrac{1.8\,{}^{\circ}\text{F}}{1.8}$

Therefore   1 BTU $= \dfrac{1.8}{0.42} \dfrac{\text{kJ}}{\text{kg} \bullet {}^{\circ}\text{C}} \times \dfrac{1 \text{ kg}}{2.20} \times \dfrac{1{}^{\circ}\text{C}}{1.8} = \underline{1.08 \text{ kJ}}$

14-53.   Heat Loss $= 0.75 \times \left(2 \text{ HP}\right) \times \left(42.4 \times 60 \dfrac{\text{BTU}}{\text{hr} \bullet \text{HP}}\right) \times \left(5 \text{ hr}\right)$

$= \underline{19,000 \text{ BTU}}$

14-54.   HP $= \dfrac{P\left(\text{psi}\right) \times Q\left(\text{gpm}\right)}{1714}$ where 1 HP $= 2544$ BTU/hr

Operating rate of high pressure PRV HP loss $= \dfrac{3000 \times 12}{1714}$

$= 21.0 \text{ HP}$

Avg rate of high press PRV HP loss $= 21.0 \text{ HP} \times \dfrac{2}{6} = 7 \text{ HP}$

Oper rate of low press PRV HP loss $= \dfrac{600 \times 12}{1714} = 4.2 \text{ HP}$

Avg rate of low press PRV HP loss $= 4.2 \text{ HP} \times \dfrac{4}{6} = 2.8 \text{ HP}$

Total average HP loss $= 7 + 2.8 = 9.8 \text{ HP}$

$= 9.8 \text{ HP} \times \dfrac{2544 \, {}^{\text{BTU}}\!/_{\text{hr}}}{1 \text{ HP}} = \underline{24,900 \, {}^{\text{BTU}}\!/_{\text{hr}}}$

14-55.   Pump Power $= \dfrac{0.020}{60} \dfrac{\text{m}^3}{\text{s}} \times 15,000 \text{ kPa} = 5 \text{ kW}$

Heat Loss $= 0.80 \times 1 \text{ kW} = 0.80 \text{ kW}$

$= 0.80 \times 60 \text{ kJ/min} = \underline{48 \text{ kJ/min}}$

14-56.   Beta ratio $= \dfrac{30,000}{1050} = \underline{28.6}$

14-57. Beta efficiency = $\dfrac{30{,}000 - 1050}{30{,}000}$ = 96.5 %

14-58. Beta efficiency = $1 - \dfrac{1}{\text{Beta ratio}}$

14-59. Identifies a particle size of 10 microns and a Beta ratio of 75 for a particular filter.

14-60. One